1·19·78

CAREER PLANNING AND PLACEMENT TODAY

CAREER
PLANNING AND
PLACEMENT
TODAY

Second Edition

C. RANDALL POWELL

**Indiana University
Graduate School of Business**

KENDALL/HUNT PUBLISHING COMPANY
2460 Kerper Boulevard, Dubuque, Iowa 52001

Ralph Crabtree strips written by:
Ronald E. Wheeler, Indiana University, Business Placement

Printed in the United States of America

401041   04

CONTENTS

2027041

PREFACE AND ACKNOWLEDGMENTS, vii

1 **CAREER PLANNING**:
Assessment—Exploration—Placement, **1**

2 **THE OUTLOOK**:
Supply—Demand—Salaries, **14**

3 **EXPLORING CAREERS**:
Environments—Structure—Positions, **25**

4 **SEARCH STRATEGY**:
Resumes—Letters—Contacts, **55**

5 **INTERVIEWING**:
Preparation—Presentation—Technique, **86**

6 **COMMUNICATIONS**:
Letters—Forms—Ethics, **107**

7 **CAREER PROGRESSION**:
Decisions—Performance—Education, **122**

EPILOGUE, 143

PREFACE AND ACKNOWLEDGMENTS

An ever-increasing supply of college graduates leads to a question of whether there will be enough jobs that require a college degree to satisfy everyone. Is the economy strong enough to absorb the increasing supply of graduates? The consensus is yes, but even the strongest optimist admits that this is a qualified yes. The supply-demand ratio is closer to equilibrium than ever before and most experts expect a tenuous balance in coming years.

A balance may be good news for employers who will have fewer problems in finding college-educated talent, but few college students or recent alumni can rejoice. A major national manpower problem may be in the offing. This book does not solve the problem, but it does address the issue for the individuals who read and use the approaches recommended.

CONCEPTS

College students can no longer concentrate their efforts on a narrow academic interest alone. The world is now more complex and requires energies to be directed to a study of a life plan rather than let fate or destiny play the sole guiding role. Career planning is nothing new but the changing economic and social environment is focusing more attention on it.

Career planning is goal directed behavior. Plan-

ning involves an introspection, an analysis of the world of work, pursuing real employment prospects, and integrating what is learned with reality. Career planning is a decision-making process that uses a series of compromises to develop a career goal and set of priorities related to long-term employment. The motivating force is career oriented employment which optimally satisfies a wide range of total life goals, attitudes, and values.

Career planning is viewed as a process that occurs over a lifetime but one which has special significance in the early stages of life, most notably in the college years.

AUDIENCE

The audience to which this book is directed includes a rather specific population. That population consists of individuals whose long-term goals relate to employment in professional, technical, managerial, or entrepreneural roles in society. Occupations clustered under these headings will likely require a college degree. The concepts relate to all academic disciplines and degree levels.

The audience is primarily college oriented but that represents a wide range of people. The concepts are applicable to high school upperclassmen and college freshmen and sophomores who are in the early stages of the career planning cycle. The motivation to get involved is somewhat higher for college juniors, seniors, and graduate students because the need to address the employment issue is closer. Early planning is most desirable but success is even possible when decisions are made late in the college study. Lastly, the concepts, methods, and techniques still may play a major role in career planning for all individuals under thirty. The ideas covered are largely entry level oriented, but experienced people often find the specific recommendations helpful.

OBJECTIVES

Over one million jobs exist for college graduates every year. There are years when the supply of graduates exceeds one million. The available opportunities go to the best qualified candidates. Who is best qualified? To some extent, this depends on the college major and degree level, but the majority of opportunities require only broadly defined skills which most graduates possess. The best qualified candidates show employers in a convincing way how and why they are most ideally suited for a given assignment. Being sincere and convincing is not an easy task. It takes the type of knowledge that this book offers.

Career Planning and Placement Today is designed to assist current students and college trained individuals in selecting, obtaining, and progressing in a career position. The career planning concepts and placement techniques give the competitive advantage needed. The ideas work for everyone and have been proven time after time in the career marketplace.

A framework is provided which is used to appraise career potential, explore career options consistent with desires, set realistic career goals, and implement a plan to satisfy career goals. Career planning greatly assists everyone who uses the approach with some expertise and understanding of its benefits and shortcomings. This approach is not a panacea for all career related problems, but it represents a collection of some of the best knowledge available from career professionals.

ACKNOWLEDGMENTS

Career Planning and Placement Today is a major revision to *Career Planning and Placement for the College Graduate of the '70's,* which was first published in 1974. The first publication went through a minor revision and several different printings as the supply of books continued to fall short of the demand. I humbly appreciate the positive reception

that the earlier work received from hundreds of colleges, students, and employers.

This edition follows the original edition, and *MBA Career Performance Ten Years After Graduation, Readings in Career Planning and Placement,* and *Business Career Guide,* all of which are now out of print. The material in this book builds upon the earlier works and hopefully adds significantly to the field. Over the years, many people and groups have had a great influence on my thinking so acknowledging everyone publicly is hardly a feasible task, but I am not any less grateful. I would be remiss, however, if I failed to acknowledge a few very special people and groups of individuals who made a unique contribution to my works.

No words can express my gratitude and respect for the late Professor J.D. Snider, my colleague and mentor for many years. Without Doug's prodding, cajoling, suggestions, and inspiration, none of the original publications would have come to fruition. Many of the concepts, strategies, and techniques owe their birth to Professor Snider, who is nationally recognized as one of the earliest deans in the profession. His philosophical thinking and gentle management style influenced my approach to the field more than any other factor. My praise for such a leader could never cease.

As the team of Snider and Powell gained recognition, another member of the team kept contributing significantly to the advancement of our efforts with little formal recognition. The person who over the years carried the team through some low as well as high points is Mrs. Frieda Robertson. Her official role as Office Manager is dwarfed in significance when compared to another role as contributor, editor, organizer, subtle critic, and friend that she played for us. I especially want to thank her for her assistance in bringing this publication together in an organized, meaningful, and timely fashion.

This edition contains several cartoon strips depicting the woes and joys of college characters as they move through the various phases of career planning and placement. The concerns and apprehension of Ralph Crabtree and friends reflect the attitudes of many college graduates. In fact, Ralph's creator recently went through the career scene at the University of Nebraska and successfully landed a job with a large American corporation. My thanks go to Ronald E. Wheeler for bringing the material to life in this unique way. Ron is truly a creative person whose energies and enthusiasms greatly aid in the understanding and appreciation of career planning.

I want to thank the thousands of students at Indiana University and Ohio State who used, abused, cussed, and discussed in my career planning courses much of the original materials in their planning and career search process. Without the feedback of these cooperative groups of conscientious students, the quality and usefulness of this approach would be far less productive for their succeeding colleagues. I hope to incorporate the comments and ideas of current students in future editions so I welcome constructive suggestions for improvement.

Writing is a lonely activity that for me requires solitude. The work in a large and active placement office does not stop when the boss decides to write a book. The office is understaffed, and the workload gets shared by considerate colleagues. Over the years I have been fortunate in having a willing staff who even encourage my absence. They tell me that they get more done when I am away! The two hundred plus graduate assistants who over the years helped fit a lot of the pieces together could hardly be individually thanked here, but their contribution was nonetheless important. The two assistants who picked up the lion's share of my work were J. Sidney Downey (now a Professor at Hope College) and Dr. Robert Greenberg, Associate Director. I thank both of them for their constructive critique and suggestions for improving the manuscript.

With thousands of the original book in circulation, almost every colleague in the career planning and placement profession has had a crack at making a contribution. The mail continues to bring in letters with both praise and criticism. I encourage everyone to write because only with this feedback can an author improve. I have tried to incorporate the many ideas, suggestions, comments, and approaches in the writing of this major revision. Another important part of our profession, employers of college graduates, regularly offer valuable inputs. The contributors from the professions are simply too numerous to individually acknowledge but their suggestions still deserve and earn my sincerest appreciation.

In the final analysis, the responsibility to organize and interpret material rests with the author. I deserve a kick where errors exist and where I have taken too many liberties in interpreting others. I accept responsibility for the shortcomings but hope that students and colleagues alike will call them to my attention. I view this book and its changes as a temporary state as I already have new plans for another revision.

Before closing, I must thank my wife Kathy and son "C.R." and closest friends (including a terribly neglected Little League Team) for putting up with me through a long summer of cloistered writing. The fun and personal rewards for me unfortunately do not impact equally upon people closest to me. Their understanding and recognition of the importance of the project is much appreciated.

C. Randall Powell, Ph.D.
Indiana University

1

CAREER PLANNING:
Assessment—Exploration—Placement

"We foresee no return to the conditions of the fifties and sixties in which employers were forced to bid against each other for the services of new college graduates." These words of former Secretary of Labor Hodgson in late 1972 should spark a note of challenge to today's graduating college students as this prediction does appear to be materializing. Assuming an imbalance in the supply of and the demand for college graduates in the next decade, what can the current graduate do to insure a professional role in our society? Many experts in higher education are convinced that one solution is sound career planning that is conducted, with guidance, by each individual graduate.

CAREER PLANNING DEFINED

Career planning is an individualized process. Each person possesses a unique set of values, philosophy, personality, interests, intelligence, and educational and work experiences. Many view the role of a professional counselor as one of assisting the individual in understanding the nature of their unique characteristics.

Career planning is more than an understanding of self. The work environment is also a key element in career planning because without an understanding of occupational alternatives, the individual is unable to effectively correlate personal characteristics with occupational realities.

Career planning is a way of thinking about the future. It is not a sterile academic exercise of matching personal characteristics and occupation in order to evolve an optimal niche for the individual. The implementation of a career plan involves the actual employment in an existing role in society. The culmination of employment in an entry-level position is only the beginning of career planning because it is a dynamic process that continues throughout life.

Objectives

This book narrows its focus to college graduates and the important career decisions most often made during the twenty-to-thirty age range.

The goals of this book are: to provide a simple framework to appraise career potential, to explore various alternatives, to implement a plan to achieve a chosen field's entry position, and to decide on the most appropriate initial employer after college that will best enhance long-term career progress. More specifically, it is directed toward the college graduate who is nearing completion of a bachelor or graduate degree program. The ideas presented apply to the recently graduated student, the military returnee, or the young person with less than five years of experience who wishes to change jobs.

The focus is on the about-to-graduate person because rarely will the opportunity again present itself to explore such a wide range of available career paths. There are far fewer hesitations from potential employers in the hiring of fresh college graduates than hiring employees on the rebound from another job.

The recent college graduate is less likely to be stereotyped by previous employment. This fact places the graduate in perhaps a more favorable employment status than at any other point in life. The occupational alternatives are broader, the employer selections more numerous, and the bargaining positions more favorable. As a result, career planning is extremely important, even essential, to the graduating college student.

Career planning concepts impact upon all graduates, regardless of their academic major. The ideas pertain equally well to persons contemplating careers in business, education, government, or not-for-profit institutions. Whether the goal is teacher, executive, entrepreneur, engineer, doctor, lawyer, performer, athlete, etc., the career planning process pulls the fibers together in a meaningful manner.

THE CAREER PLANNING PROCESS

According to Mark Twain, "the happiest and most successful person works all year long at what he would otherwise choose to do on his summer vacation." Voltaire acknowledged that "work alone makes life bearable, keeps away boredom, vice and need." One might conclude that to achieve some success and happiness, each individual should work at something that makes full use of the interests, aptitudes, and other personal characteristics of that individual.

The first step begins with a self-assessment which provides answers to the basic questions.

What do I want to do?
What can I do?
What needs to be done?

Career planning is a continuous process that occurs over a lifetime. Career planning is not limited solely to analyzing the work setting because life-style and other interests often override practical job related concerns. Planning cannot be done in a sterile fixed environment because the multitude of factors needing to be considered are constantly in a state of flux.

Getting a handle on the variables relating to career planning is difficult but not impossible. Completion of a college degree program is frequently one of the major transitions in a person's life. "Where to after college?" is more than a cliche!

Certain decisions impacting upon the future are imminent. Most graduates recognize that the status quo cannot or should not last much longer. Career planning represents a decision-making sequence of events. The decisions involved in career planning require the same approach as any action oriented decision-making process. The process usually revolves around the five decision-making steps shown in Figure 1-1.

DECISION-MAKING STEPS

1. Define the problem
2. Develop alternatives
3. Evaluate alternatives
4. Make decisions
5. Revise decisions

Figure 1-1.

Self-assessment

The overall goal in career decision making is to obtain a career position consistent with academic training, past experiences (work and life), personality, abilities, aptitudes, values, interests, etc. Most people do not know where they stand in relation to these variables. The factors related to background characteristics are difficult to evaluate. Even if such factors can be identified and evaluated, the project is not always fun.

The essence of career planning is merging information related to a person and information related to a career. Logical reasoning demands that sound decisions on career/life planning can only be possible if facts about the two parts are available.

The process of developing information about the person is known as "self-assessment." The inclusion of the word "self" implies that the final "putting it together" must be completed by the person involved. Help in laying out the framework and the approach may require the help of others.

Career Exploration

The process of developing information about the career alternatives can best be described as "career exploration." The term implies that there is a wealth of information about nearly every career field, but unfortunately the data is not all located in one or two convenient sources. As the word "exploration" suggests, digging into a mass of information is often necessary in order to cull out the most pertinent information.

Integration

Assuming success in collecting information on self and several career fields, the next step requires integrating the information. The frustrating integration process demands perseverance because the pieces rarely fit neatly together. The integration turns out to be a compromise process. Trade-offs become the norm.

A sorting begins to occur in the career planning decision-making process. This sorting out often continues well after a career path has been charted. The end result of this integrating process is a definitively stated career objective. Career goals need to be formulated in such a manner that permits them to be communicated to others.

Placement

The "placement function" then begins to emerge in the career planning process. Placement provides the road map. The placement function continues to serve as a feedback loop that reinforces or alters the career goals established earlier. Placement represents the portion of the career planning cycle which is closely linked with testing earlier decisions through a real world exposure.

The career planning cycle is depicted in Figure 1-2 as an integrated approach to career planning.

Career Planning Cycle

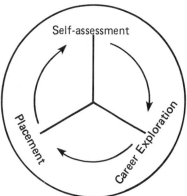

Figure 1-2.

The wheel will be difficult to roll if one of the edges falls flat. This does not mean that someone cannot be successful in a career if these components are not all present. Before the major shifts in the economy took place in the late sixties and seventies, there were enough career options available that people could be successful without a plan. Times change.

VOCATIONAL THEORIES

Career planning is not without some theory based referents. Considerable research in the field of career guidance and vocational theory supports the dynamics of the relationships. Theory is more a subject for guidance counselors but it is the rare college student who does not come into contact with the career counseling professional. Consequently, it is important to recognize and appreciate the foundation upon which their advice is built.

The professional counselor can be extremely valuable in helping assess and evaluate an individual's capability and in providing guidance and referral to related career resources. Their work is tied to research by theorists that relate to several decades of analysis.

Many people start to think about what they want to do as a vocation early in life, often before the teens. A great many personal factors, in addition to external forces, appear to influence the various career related choices that are made. Theories range from astrological happenings to paternal handling of young children. The widest accepted theories are known as developmental theories of vocational choices.

Why is a vocational theory important? A vocational theory is important because it helps to understand the how and why of certain life sequences that assist in the selection of an appropriate occupational endeavor. A theory shows a systematic relationship between certain variables and helps define relevancy.

A theory develops a system of classification and structuring of concepts that can be used to predict facts. A good theory is most often based on extensive empirical referents which means that the propositions in a theory are logically supported by prior research and/or experience.

Two of the more practical theories are briefly summarized here for the purpose of helping to see how a professional counselor would analyze vocational behavior. All of these theories are developmental in nature. They view vocational choices as a process that occurs over a time sequence.

Ginzberg's Theory

Dr. Eli Ginzberg and his colleagues at Columbia first proposed their theory of occupational choice in 1951. Their theory attempted to explain how the multiplicity of factors within the environment and forces within the individual act and react on each other so that individuals could finally resolve the problem of their vocational choice. Three major concepts in Ginzberg's theory form the vocational choice framework: process, irreversibility, and compromise.

Vocational development is a process because it changes over time, and these time periods may be

---

GINZBERG THEORY BASICS

1. Vocational development is a process
2. The choice is largely irreversible
3. The choice represents a compromise

Figure 1-3.

delineated into various life stages. The first stage is a "fantasy stage" (before age 11) where children believe they can become whatever they desire. The next stage is a "tentative stage" (age 11-17) in which the young adult begins to develop a set of values, interests, qualifications, and personality. Choices often evolve and change during this second stage.

The final stage is described as a "realistic stage" in which the individual begins to integrate interests, capabilities, and values. These factors are used to evaluate the real environment, a process that can be expressed into three periods—exploration, crystallization, and specification. In the exploration period, individuals acquaint themselves for the last time with career alternatives in a highly realistic context. During crystallization, clear vocational patterns begin to form based upon the successes and failures experienced in the exploration period. Choice follows. During specification the individual delimits the choice and elaborates by selecting a specific career, college major, or graduate school specialty. During the college years, many students roam through these three periods before deciding on a specific career direction.

Ginzberg sees the choice as being largely irreversible because reality pressures introduce major obstacles. After a major commitment, such as the decision to pursue a career in teaching or in law, there are often serious emotional barriers to a shift in plans because this change can take on the quality of failure or at least present a threat to self-esteem.

The third major concept in Ginzberg's theory is that the vocational choice represents a compromise. The individual tries to choose a career that can make as much use as possible of personal interests and abilities in a manner that will satisfy the most values and goals. The person must weigh the opportunities and environmental limitations and then assess the extent to which a maximum degree of satisfaction in work and life can be secured. The individual attempts to balance abilities, interests, and values against real environment career alternatives and thus make appropriate compromises.

As a whole, Ginzberg's theory has weathered well through extensive empirical research.

Holland's Theory

Another developmental theory of vocational choice is that expounded by Dr. John L. Holland in 1966. Holland suggests that career choices represent an extension of broad behavioral styles in the context of one's life work. He proposes that individuals develop a certain "modal personal orientation" as a result of their interests, personality, values, and patterns of ability. He classifies these "personal orienta-

tions" into six major areas and also classifies "occupational environments" into six major American work categories. Certain personal orientations can be characterized in each of the six occupational environments, thus providing a relationship between the individual's personal orientation and work environments.

People tend to project views of themselves and views of the world of work onto occupational titles. Holland analyzes and classifies over 300 occupational titles into one of the six occupational environments. Through such techniques of introspection, self-evaluation, and psychological testing, individuals can be placed in one of the six personal orientations and, therefore, be matched with a basic occupational environment. Individuals making the vocational choice search for the work environment that satisfies their personal orientations.

Holland also proposed that self-knowledge operates to increase or decrease the accuracy with which a person makes a vocational choice. This leads to two major hypotheses which he has empirically supported.

1. Persons with inaccurate self-knowledge make inadequate choices more frequently than do persons with more accurate self-appraisals.
2. Persons with more information about occupational environments make more adequate choices than do persons with less information.

Thus Holland concludes that a person's vocational behavior can be explained by the interaction of the modal personal orientation and the occupational environment. The adequacy of this choice relates to the level of self-knowledge and the level of occupational knowledge.

Theory Summary

Although there are a number of other important theories of vocational choice, these two theories can serve to provide the needed concepts for understanding the importance of early career planning. Ginzberg's theory should help to understand where the individual presently is in the vocational development process and what compromises will likely be necessary. Holland's theories stress the importance of making an accurate self-concept and emphasize that a high level of occupational knowledge is needed before making a sound decision.

SELF-ASSESSMENT

Sound career decisions come only after a thorough analysis of one's total background. Liter-

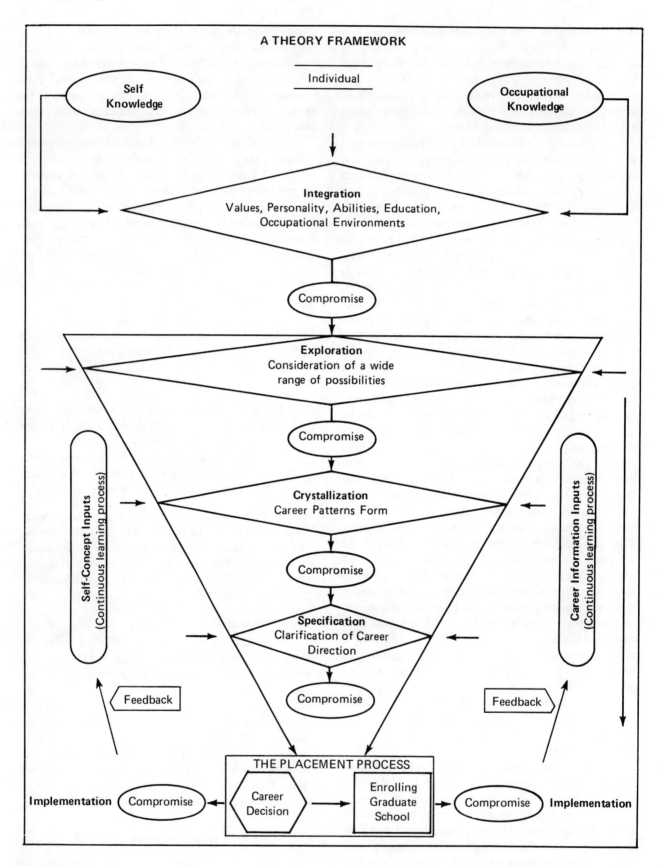

Figure 1-4.

ally hundreds of variables interact together to produce a distinct and unique individual. A reasonable classification scheme might include the variables and categories described as ''Ten Personal Assessors'' in Figure 1-5.

Most people find it very difficult to write even a three-page paper identifying the subcomponents of each of the ten personal assessors. Education and work history are rather straightforward, but the others demand some deep thought.

Interestingly, it is the other eight factors that potential employers try hardest to determine from an interview. Very few of the personal assessors even appear on a resume and yet they are the factors having the most direct bearing on an individual's ability to accomplish many jobs at the professional and managerial level.

Isn't it surprising that many college graduates seeking their first job after college—the most transitional stage in life—barge into the placement stage of career planning without thoroughly investigating themselves and the options open to them? Directly or indirectly, employers evaluate each of the ten personal assessors and develop an image of the job candidate. Placement directors find it interesting to hear recruiters discuss candidates in some detail while the candidate has never thought about him or herself in similar terms.

Often the employer's analysis is far off base. How could the validity ever be high if the candidate has not conducted a self-interview before the job interview? Through intentional and unintentional verbal or nonverbal cues, job candidates relay to employers information about themselves. This information is valuable only if the candidate knows the subject matter.

Whether the information transmitted is accurate or not, the employer processes it as truth. Many graduates are rejected for jobs for which—if the truth were known—they are eminently qualified but they failed to communicate an accurate picture of their background. Conversely, many graduates get jobs for which they are not qualified and subsequently fail on the job because they, too, transmitted a convincing yet inaccurate picture of their background. The job candidate and employer come out losers in both situations.

The solution to the problem is simple. Employers are becoming trained and more proficient at evaluating job candidates. Job candidates must become more proficient at communicating the truth. This does not add up to interview coaching, polishing, and/or deceptive packaging. The solution for job candidates requires getting into the fundamentals of career planning and not superficial window dressing. The basics of career planning are self-assessment, career exploration, and placement in that order. The structure of this book follows those three simple principles.

TEN PERSONAL ASSESSORS

Educational Experiences

Work History

Interests

Aspirations

Special Abilities

Aptitudes

Personal Qualities

Attitudes

Personal Values

Personality

Figure 1-5.

Conducting the Self-assessment

There is no one best way to conduct a self-assessment. Most college placement counselors offer assistance in this analysis. A wide array of publications, often in workbook format, are available in public and university libraries and bookstores. Many career counseling and placement officers on campus offer psychological tests to aid in the assessment. With all of the assistance available, the key word to remember is "self" because the final analysis must be conducted by the person.

Self-assessment is a do-it-yourself project. Although the final result may be a private matter between the person and a professional counselor, information should be drawn from friends, past employers, parents, faculty, neighbors, clergy, etc. If inquiries are properly phrased, great insights can be gained from others.

The self-assessment must be written on paper, not just stored in an unorganized fashion in one's mind. Unlike a resume which is designed to appeal and sell, the self-assessment reveals personal attributes that rarely can be articulated in a humble way. A fair and honest evaluation shows weaknesses as well as strengths. Understanding liabilities as well as assets aids in the merging process between self-information and career information.

Autobiography

Most self-assessment projects or exercises fall into three general categories as shown in Figure 1-6. The autobiography method is written in an organized prose style. The biography may be a chronological listing of all major events in one's life or take the approach of being organized around topical headings such as education, work experiences, activities, hobbies, special skills, honors, leadership roles, etc. It

would be appropriate to use the "Ten Personal Assessors" as topical headings.

One important take-off on the autobiography is to develop a general life plan for the future. The idea is not necessarily to lay out specific career fields but to chart general life guidelines relative to such factors as monetary expectations, life-style, family, personal values, etc.

Inventory

The inventory represents a checklist approach to identifying the personal assessors. Career workbooks and counselors often provide lists of questions to answer, descriptive adjectives to check, list of skills to identify, common values to appraise, and personality scales to evaluate. Essentially, the inventory provides a classification system. Again, the purpose is to draw out specific strengths and weaknesses which can be used to understand questions more related to the "why" of personal actions.

Psychological Testing

Psychological tests provide information about certain characteristics that individuals possess. Tests may be used by an employer or school to predict future performance. Although tests are still widely used by schools and government agencies, its use as a selection tool for professional and managerial positions in business and industry appears to be waning.

METHODS OF SELF-ASSESSMENT
Autobiography
Inventory
Psychological Testing

Figure 1-6.

The use of testing by career counselors is designed to provide knowledge about one's self which can be related to specific occupations. By sharing the results of a test instrument with a counselee, the information adds to the base of knowledge about self in an organized manner.

Career counselors provide a professional interpretation of the results of testing but still leave the decision on career choice up to the client. Testing does not give decisions. Tests provide a multidimensional array of personal information and the counselor offers guidance to avenues which might be fruitful to explore.

Types of Tests

Career counselors typically administer five major types of tests shown in Figure 1-7. These five types of standardized tests provide a significant

PSYCHOLOGICAL TESTS	
Type of Test	**Measures**
Intelligence	Abstract reasoning and capacity for mastering problems
Achievement	Extent of knowledge in a given field
Aptitude	Potential for acquiring specific types of knowledge
Interest	Stock taking of likes, dislikes, and skills
Personality	Emotional makeup, stability, and adjustment

Figure 1-7.

amount of useful information assuming described rules in administration, scoring under definite rules, and interpretation with reference to a norm group. The extent to which a test accurately measures a given variable (validity) is supported by extensive research. Their reliability (consistency on repeated administrations) is statistically proven. Although tests are not infallible, one should assess the results with a high level of credibility.

EXPLORATION

One of the most frequent questions fielded by college placement officers is "What job possibilities are available for someone with my background?" One of the first questions asked by an employer is "For what position are you applying and what qualifies you for it?" Graduates are wise in asking the first question of the placement officer because if it was asked of the employer, in most cases, they would be out the door as fast as they arrived.

Even at the senior year, most students do not know what they want to do in a specific way. Even many graduates with specific vocationally related majors like accounting, engineering, journalism, etc., are not sure. Many students during the freshman, sophomore, and junior years are more concerned about passing courses and Saturday night than with their long-term career plans. A trend is developing for students to become more career oriented earlier but times change slowly.

At some point in a college career, most students begin to think about work after college. With some, the concern starts as a freshman and in others it comes in the last semester of the final year. From the career counselor's perspective, the earlier . . . the better. The last term of the final year is much too late, but even then, all is not lost. There are differences in the philosophy about why people go to college.

The career planning process (assessment—exploration—placement) can occur at any period in time. The process can be condensed into four weeks or expanded into four years. Logic suggests that the longer the time frame, the better the refinement and integration with reality.

Career exploration is a process designed to accumulate information about the world of work. The goal is to create a high level of awareness about many different career alternatives. The process may collect data as specific as a job in a given organization or as general as a broad definition. The actual method, however, involves an in-depth investigation into a given career option which can be repeated with other career options.

People collect career information all the time. Simply by observing a medical center television program, information is collected. Every day people are observed in action in various occupations and that information is mentally processed. Unfortunately, not all information processed is accurate. Inexact data can be worse than no information if career decisions are based upon it.

Career information exists in many places in several forms. Career information presents problems when not displayed in a logical format. Bits and pieces here and there seldom add up to sound data

unless recorded on paper in a useable form. The data must be summed up in a manner that can aid in the clarification of career objectives. In the final analysis, the information will be an essential ingredient of the interviewing phase of the placement function.

In collecting information a systematic approach expedites the process. A scheme depicted in Figure 1-8 can be helpful in sorting out relevant from irrelevant information. Searching for specific data on a given career field permits one to scan a much greater volume of work.

The *Dictionary of Occupational Titles* (DOT) published by the Government Printing Office lists over 35,000 job titles. Different titles can relate to similar duties because titles and descriptions are not universally accepted. For example, the job titles of financial analyst, budget specialist, cost accountant, and credit analyst could all have the same description of duties. Job titles are not as descriptive as they could be so one should not rely on titles alone to give an idea of the job content.

Job descriptions vary in content from employer to employer, but most give a summary of the job and list various duties and responsibilities. A job description indicates what, how, and why the employee does on the job. It also gives various reporting relation-

---

CAREER INFORMATION

Titles

Description

Duties/Responsibilities

Qualifications

Outlook

Training

Advancement

Figure 1-8.

---

ships which can be helpful in tracking a potential career path.

Many individuals in assessing career information find it helpful to investigate the chances and routes for upward mobility. Some jobs lend themselves to mobility more than others. The need for advancement is more important to some people than others. For some professionals, such as professors, veterinarians, and doctors, advancement is almost defined out of the job. In contrast, the manager in business continues to strive for promotions.

Jobs vary in their ability to provide an element of training other than on-the-job training. Some offer formal sophisticated training opportunities while others are fairly structured and routinized. For individuals desiring training opportunities, this type of career information often makes the decision.

The number of people needed in various occupations and specific jobs is an important factor to evaluate. There are very few astronomers and many teachers, and thus landing a job teaching may be somewhat easier than finding work as an astronomer. The supply/demand ratio is another factor related to career outlook that needs evaluation.

Sources

People and publications provide the basic sources of career information. People in occupations and career positions serve as role models to which potential aspirants might relate. Much of career knowledge comes simply by observing people in their day-to-day life-style. But appearances can be deceiving so observation cannot alone be the primary source of career knowledge.

Interviewing people in selected career fields provides a real world appreciation of the duties and responsibilities within the assignment. One or two opinions in a field, however, can be misleading be-

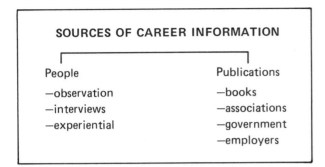

Figure 1-9.

cause practitioners are often biased. It takes care to see through the enthusiasm and pride to get into the bad points as well as the pluses.

Perhaps the one best way to learn about an occupation is to work with people in the field as a subprofessional through a cooperative education or professional practice program. A ten to fifteen week work experience usually permits one to see most aspects of the field. The trend to using these experiential types of programs appear to be growing so that this may be more of an option for more people in the future.

Publications

Everyone is not fortunate enough to have the opportunity to observe, act, and react with people in careers in which they have an interest. In such instances, one must turn to written documents. In some ways, publications are superior to personal interaction because the information is more broad based. Most publications are written only after taking observations from large numbers of people in the occupation rather than relying on only two or three opinions.

Public and university libraries contain hundreds of books on many different career fields. The card catalog is the place to start.

Most professional associations publish books, booklets, and pamphlets about careers. Although libraries contain some of these, it is appropriate to write associations directly. Many college placement officers maintain supplies to give away.

The U.S. Government also prints similar types of information which is available in libraries, college placement offices, or from the Government Printing Office. The most useful of the government publications which should be reviewed by every college student is the *Occupational Outlook Handbook for College Graduates,* which is published periodically. It gives a brief description and the current outlook for nearly every position sought by college students.

Most large employers of college graduates whether business, government, or education publish employment brochures that describe career opportunities for college graduates with their organization. Although one sometimes must read through the sales pitch, these brochures often give the most up-to-date description of career fields. The brochures are available from college placement offices and by writing organizations directly.

Systematic Exploration

Information about most careers is available, but it often takes some digging to collect the required data even if one knows exactly what type of information for which to search. Because of this a consistent methodology needs to be developed.

A systematic way is needed to collect, process, and evaluate the information with the express goal of making career decisions based upon the information. Not all bits of the research effort will be of significant value and, in fact, some of the researched data will be worthless because it may have been proven false by other research. Some career information writers have greater credibility than others.

Most college students spend hundreds of hours researching and writing term papers during their college years. The one project that is probably as important to the student's future as any other is the career exploration project. The hours invested in career exploration should exceed those invested in any other college subject. Yet, some graduates leave college each year without having invested even ten hours in a project around which their entire working lives may revolve. The overriding reason given for not doing it is because it was not required by a college professor!

The timing of the systematic exploration is not critical. The first phase (collecting) may well begin before college and continue through the last year of a program. A point in time, however, needs to be set aside to do some stock taking, and one ideal point is the beginning of the last year of a college program. The motivation and career interest levels begin to peak about this time.

The key to systematic exploration is writing the information in a form that can be processed. Information flows from a variety of sources and in varying quantity, quality, and format. The data is cleaned, filtered, and arranged to achieve a logical order that can be manipulated.

Career information is evaluated. The purpose of the evaluation or review is to make some decision using the data collected. This evaluation occurs in the frame of reference of the self-assessment completed earlier. The evaluation represents an integration of

hundreds of variables and related parts from both the self-assessment and the exploration.

Most individuals face important compromises during this integrating process. Some refuse to compromise between reality and fantasy. Others restart the career information collection process as they reject the career field. Still others rethink through the self-assessment process.

In the end, some type of decision filters out. The decision becomes the career objective statement on a resume. After the career objective statement, focus centers on several appropriate entry-level assignments. The placement function is close to being utilized although there still may be further specification and clarification of career interest. In practice, the clarifications continue throughout the placement process.

PLACEMENT

The term "placement" is a misnomer. It implies to the applicant that of the hundreds of job openings available, a super power in the form of an emissary will select the most ideal job and give it to the applicant. Few job manipulating godfathers exist.

Placement is an energy consuming process.

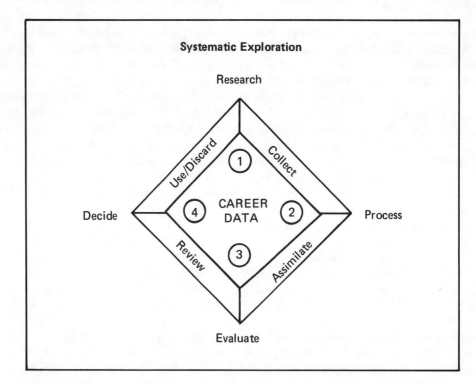

Figure 1-10.

Without proper advance planning, placement can destroy the spirit, will, and motivation of a job applicant. The mechanics of placement come only after a well-conceived plan that integrates self-assessment with career alternatives. Placement begins with a clearly defined set of career objectives. Without a high level of career direction, placing the placement process in gear is analogous to starting a trip without a road map. A lot of expensive energy burns up and important contacts destroyed before the destination is reached.

The elements in the placement process include tools, contacts, interviews, and time. The two essential tools are the personal resume and cover letter. Both tools revolve around a distinctive statement of career aspirations.

Job campaigns rarely succeed without a source of job leads. Job leads emerge from a source of contacts which make up the backbone of the job search. The contact list of potential employment prospects derive from college placement staff recommendations, campus recruiters, faculty, and friends. Classified advertisement and employment directories form a less personal, hence less effective, source of job contacts.

Contacts represent a list of limited commodities which are consumed in the placement process. Once the contact is utilized, the bullet is spent and recharging an expended shell takes more time than pulling the trigger initially.

Another element in the placement process is the job interviews. No one obtains employment without an interview. Contacts help obtain interviews, but seldom do contacts get anyone a job. Once a negative response is given to an applicant, seldom is there a second chance for reconsideration. Interviews demand advance preparation, a well conceived strategy in the approach, and use of effective techniques to be successful.

Finally, the placement process is time and decision oriented. Success depends upon career goals matching job requirements. Without compromise, the match may never occur. Employment calls for a firm decision at a given point in time. Time pressures force career choices. Time places pressure on the need for compromise. A preplanned time and decision framework permits a rational placement process based upon a realistic assessment of the current work environment.

Placement must be viewed in the total framework of the career planning process. A runaway placement strategy is for fools only. It connotates getting a job at any cost and taking whatever is available.

Jumping into the placement function without the prior assessment and exploration phases of career planning is like entering the "Indy 500" with a passenger car. The race may be completed, but the well-designed and engineered race cars with experienced drivers will finish far sooner. It does not pay to come in last.

PLACEMENT PROCESS

Resumes	Interviews
Letters	Offers
Contacts	Job/Career

Figure 1-11.

SUMMARY

Career planning is a process. The process involves self-assessment, career exploration, and job placement. The process occurs in an integrative decision-making framework based on established time constraints which force compromises. Career planning concepts result from developmental theories or career choice. Methods of conducting the three processes were briefly discussed.

2

THE OUTLOOK:
Supply — Demand — Salaries

A college degree no longer guarantees employment. The projected supply of college graduates is expected to exceed demand for them through the mid-1980s. The rapid rise in the educational level of all college age youths (nearly one-half) grew faster than the economy's ability to absorb graduates in college level type of jobs.

The job outlook by occupation is one of the variables that the college graduate must factor into a career decision. The job outlook, however, must not become the overriding variable. There are jobs available in almost every field. The time an individual takes to identify entry-level openings and convince an employer to hire may be disproportionate to the level of interest in the job.

The relationship between supply and demand necessarily influences career decisions. No prudent individual permits supply/demand relationships to dictate a career choice; yet, the prudent person cannot afford to stand naive to the complex and uncertain characteristics of supply and demand factors generated by changing market conditions. The analysis of the marketplace necessarily becomes part of the career planning process.

Estimates of graduate supply or jobs vary considerably from year to year. The economic state of the nation influences both estimates sharply. Figures shown in this chapter may easily vary 10%, up or down, during a given period. For career planning purposes, one must assume that the estimates are "close" to the projected target and plan accordingly.

SUPPLY OF GRADUATES

Colleges continue to turn out record numbers of graduates. Current projections estimate that the next decade will graduate 50% more degree holders than the number conferred the preceding decade. There are more college age youth and an increasing percentage of them decide to attend college.

Not all 1.4 million graduates enter the labor market each year. Some continue to graduate study,

PROJECTED COLLEGE DEGREES TO BE AWARDED ANNUALLY		
Bachelor	1,036,000	72%
Master	327,000	22%
Doctorate	36,000	2%
Professional	64,000	4%
Total	1,463,000	100%
Source: National Center for Educational Statistics.		

Figure 2-1.

travel, military, marry, or otherwise decide not to accept employment. Conversely, college graduates enter the labor market from military separations, migrants, and other sources. The U.S. Bureau of Labor statistics estimates the number of college graduates entering the labor market as 1.2 million per year.

In addition to analyzing the aggregate supply of college graduates, another issue relates to the concentration of academic major subject fields of college graduates. Many occupations require specific fields of study. Humanities graduates show little inclination toward engineering oriented work assignments. If the number of jobs and graduates balanced perfectly, a major problem might still exist because the mix of candidate qualifications may not match the occupational job requirements. Consequently, because of the "mix," some graduates might go unemployed even in a boom economy.

Certain major subjects relate more to a given occupation. At many colleges a decided shift toward vocationally related majors appears to be a trend. Only a few years ago, less than 12% of college students elected to major in business versus over 16% today. In a free society, the only factors dictating a college major are the interest of the individual student and the resources of the institution. The job market might temporarily influence the selection but given a minimum of 4 years lead time and the uncertainties of the economy, few students base a college major entirely on job possibilities. It is, however, becoming one of the many factors that students use in selecting a college major.

As Figure 2-3 shows, more than half of the projected degree holders elect to major in a subject major where the potential for employment is less than favorable. Many people believe that the concept of higher education is primarily to develop the whole individual. Less concern should be placed on the academic major. The concept says that if the individual is properly prepared, the person can adapt to the work environment with a minimum of difficulty.

Whatever a person's point of view, few argue with the importance of collecting career information and permitting choice to be influenced by the research data.

OCCUPATIONAL OUTLOOK

The occupational mix of the United States economy changes daily but four major categories of workers—white-collar, blue-collar, service, and farm workers—are likely to continue. The majority of college graduates tend to work in the white-collar category and more specifically as professionals, technicians, managers, administrators, and sales pro-

---

ESTIMATED SUPPLY OF COLLEGE GRADUATES

(Bachelor, Master, and Doctorate Degrees
Expected to be Granted Each Year Through 1985)

More jobs than graduates:

Business	144,000
Computer sciences	4,000
Physical sciences	32,000
Engineering	70,000
Health services	32,000
Professions (M.D., D.D.S.)	38,000
	320,000

Jobs and graduates about equal:

Agriculture	16,000
Architecture	7,000
Biological sciences	45,500
Home economics	1,000
Library sciences	8,000
Mathematics	31,000
Public affairs	18,000
	126,500

More graduates than jobs:

Area studies	3,500
Communications	12,000
Education	270,000
Law	19,000
Letters	88,000
Psychology	44,000
Fine arts	37,500
Languages	25,600
Social sciences	175,400
Other	17,000
	692,000

Source: *Digest of Educational Statistics.*

Figure 2-3.

PROJECTED COLLEGE GRADUATES ENTERING LABOR MARKET ANNUALLY

New college graduates	989,000
Military separation	20,000
Reentrants, immigrants, etc.	183,000
Total	1,192,000

Source: U.S. Bureau of Labor Statistics.

Figure 2-2.

EMPLOYMENT OF COLLEGE GRADUATES
(1974) (in thousands)

Government (36%)	4,600
Service industries (46%)	
Retail/Wholesale trade	1,100
Service/Miscellaneous	3,600
Transportation/Utilities	340
Finance/Insurance/Real estate	880
Goods producing (18%)	
Manufacturing	1,800
Agriculture	200
Construction	235
Mining	80
Total	12,835

Figure 2-4.

PROJECTED ANNUAL OPENINGS
FOR COLLEGE GRADUATES

Growth	318,000	28%
Replacement	564,000	51%
Upgrading	227,000	21%
Total	1,109,000	100%

Figure 2-5.

fessionals. By 1985, white-collar workers will make up more than one-half of the total employment.

Approximately one-fifth of all jobs require persons who have completed four or more years of college compared to only 10% in 1960. College graduates fill 75% of all jobs in the professional and technical occupations and one-half of the openings in managerial and administrative occupations.

The local, state, and federal government employs about one-third of college educated persons. In private industry, service-producing industries employ the largest number of college graduates. Goods-producing industries employ about one-fifth of all college educated persons. The fast growing service industry includes industries such as business services, health care, domestic services, maintenance and repair, advertising, recreation, retail trade, wholesale trade, transportation, finance, insurance, real estate, etc.

The service producing industries are expected to contribute twice as much to growth in employment than goods producing industries. The public sector is expected to increase employment of college graduates by about 3% per year and the private sector about 2% per year. For college graduates, employment within the various sectors of the labor market should follow past growth patterns.

Contributing Growth Factors

Job openings for college graduates entering the labor force are expected to be approximately 1.1 million per year. Slightly over half of the openings will result from replacement of college graduates who die, retire, or leave the work force. Growth in em-

ployment is expected to represent 28% and 21% will come from jobs not previously requiring a college degree.

The Job Gap

The increase in the number of college level jobs falls short of the number of graduates on an annualized basis. This anlysis projects an oversupply of 100,000 college graduates each year. Over 1.2 million graduates (including labor market dropouts and re-entrants) will chase 1.1 million job openings each year. Of course, there will be major variances each year depending upon the actual number graduating (influenced by birth rates and ability to pass courses) and the national economic situation. In selected parts of the nation there could also be major dislocations resulting from local situations.

The job gap translates into "underemployment" more than unemployment for college graduates. Because of training, maturity, communication skills, etc., employers will hire graduates for tasks for which a college degree is not required and thus not fully utilize the graduate's capabilities.

The job gap compounds major national problems. As college graduates spill over into blue-collar and clerical jobs, entry-level jobs for less educated persons disappear. Individuals already on the lower economic rung get pushed further down and higher unemployment among those less prepared to economically cope with it results.

Another issue relates to the college graduates previously forced into these jobs during the economic recessions of the seventies. Will employers promote them? Are they unhappy? Will promotion siphon even more jobs from the current graduating class?

Over the next decade the "college job gap" is likely to have an adverse effect on those with less education. Opportunity to advance for workers without a college degree is severely restrained. As the large pool of post-World War II baby boom people (now in their thirties and moving into middle and top management) progress, fewer opportunities for advancement may be available to current graduates. It

may be prudent for government and private employers to moderate the fast track upward mobility concept and promote more rotational assignments to give variety in career fields.

Occupational Projections

Accurate projections of specific occupational job openings on an annual basis creates problems. Accuracy eludes the best researcher because of the technological and societal environmental changes. But, people thirst for general guidelines. Guidelines help planning but to use them with any fevor invites trouble.

With that caveat, detailed projections for a selected number of occupations traditionally requiring a college degree are presented in Figure 2-6. The list includes some occupations for which a college degree may not be a requirement. Many college graduates may accept jobs in these fields as employers attempt to upgrade the educational level of their employees. The list does not include a number of skilled blue-collar occupations or clerical type of positions that graduates might accept.

The sources for the occupational trends and prospect projections are based on two publications from the U.S. Department of Labor: *Occupational Outlook Handbook in Brief* and *Occupational Manpower and Training Needs* (1824). A job description for each occupation is available in the *Occupational Outlook Handbook*.

The "growth trend" column is based upon the percentage of increase/decrease in the number of people employed in the occupation in 1974 compared to projections in 1985:

A = Change of greater than 45%
B = 35-44% growth rate
C = 25-34% growth rate
D = 15-24% growth rate
F = Less than 14% rate of growth

The "competitive prospects" column is based upon an estimate of the supply/demand ratio. Many occupations correlate directly with academic subjects in which case a fairly accurate estimate of supply is available. Other occupations have no correlatable major in which case a reasonable estimate is made based on past trends. In a small way, the column gives the individual an estimate of chances to get into the field: the higher the grade, the more competition faced so the higher his/her credentials must be. The grade scale might translate:

A = Excellent chances; many more jobs than graduates
B = Very good chances; more jobs than graduates
C = Average prospects; job/graduate ratio about equal
D = Keen competition; more graduates than jobs

Summary

Each person makes a career decision based upon all available information collected. Decisions cannot be based solely upon any one factor such as immediate job prospects. Jobs exist in every occupation. The methods used to obtain the job may require hard work and much time. Nonetheless, a challenge should not deter one from going after the career prospect that best matches abilities, qualifications, and interests. A prudent course of action is to strive for several job possibilities simultaneously and to keep a fall-back position in mind as a compromise.

Researching job prospects is part of the career exploration process. Without inserting this real world element into the career planning equation, one risks major problems. The placement phase of career planning often becomes nothing more than a fantasy ego destroying process as one turndown gets heaped upon another if the exploration is not conducted.

OCCUPATIONAL TRENDS AND PROSPECTS

Occupation	Average Annual Job Opening	Growth Trends	Competitive Prospects
Accountants	45,500	D+	B+
Actuaries	700	C+	D
Administrators			
College	5,800	A+	B
Elem/Secondary	13,700	C+	C
Health service	17,400	A+	A
Medical record	1,100	C	A
Air traffic controllers	750	D+	D
Airline pilots	2,800	C	C
Anthropologists	250	B+	D
Architects	3,000	A	C
Architects: Landscape	900	A	A
Archivists/Curators	525	B	C
Artists: Commercial	4,000	D+	D
Astronomers	30	F	D
Bank officer	16,000	B	C+
Broadcast technicians	1,350	D	C
Buyers (ind/retail)	9,000	B	C
Chemists	6,400	C	B
Chiropractors	1,200	D+	B
City managers	150	A	D
Claim representative	6,600	D+	D
Clergy	10,600	F	D
Computer programmers	13,000	B+	B
Computer systems analysts	9,100	A+	B+
Computer specialists	1,200	A+	B+
Construction inspectors	1,700	B+	B
Counselor: College	250	D+	D
Counselor: Employment	650	A	D
Counselor: Rehabilitation	2,100	A	B
Counselor: School	2,050	F	D
Credit managers	4,500	B	B
Dental hygienists	6,300	A+	A
Dentists	6,200	C+	B
Designers: Industrial	450	D	D
Designers: Interior	1,550	D	D
Dietitians	3,200	C	C
Drafters	17,300	B+	B

Occupation	Average Annual Job Opening	Growth Trends	Competitive Prospects
Economists	4,700	A	D
Engineers:			
Aerospace	1,100	F	C
Agriculture	550	C+	B
Biomedical	150	C+	B
Ceramic	550	C+	B
Chemical	1,850	C	B
Civil	9,300	B	B
Electrical	12,200	C+	B
Industrial	7,200	C	B
Mechanical	7,900	C	B
Metallurgical	550	D+	C
Mining	350	B+	B
Petroleum	750	A	B
Engr. technicians	45,800	B+	B
Farm managers	70	F	F
Foresters	950	D+	D
Forest technicians	500	C+	D
Geographers	650	B+	C
Geologists	1,300	B	B
Geophysicists	450	B	B
Health inspectors	7,900	B+	B
Health technicians	12,800	A+	A
Historians	1,300	D	D
Home management advisors	500	D	D
Hotel managers/ Assistants	6,500	D+	C
Insurance representatives	19,400	D	C
Interpreters	50	F	F
Judges	1,350	D	D
Lawyers	26,400	B+	D
Librarians	10,400	D+	C
Market research workers	3,000	A	C
Mathematicians	1,550	D	D
Math technicians	50	B+	B
Medical laboratory technicians	18,800	B+	B
Merchant marine	150	F	F
Meteorologists	200	D+	C

Figure 2-6.

OCCUPATIONAL TRENDS AND PROSPECTS (cont.)

Occupation	Average Annual Job Opening	Growth Trends	Competitive Prospects
Newspaper reporters	2,200	F	C
OSHA workers	1,100	C	C
Oceanographers	100	D+	D
Operations analysts	7,900	A+	A
Optometrists	900	D+	B
Personnel	23,000	B+	D
Pharmacists	6,500	D	B
Physicians	23,000	A	B
Physicists	1,700	C	B
Podiatrists	400	D	B
Police officers	22,000	B	B
Police (state)	3,600	A+	B
Psychologists	5,200	B+	B
Public relations assistant	6,500	C	D
Purchasing agents	11,700	B	B
Radio and TV announcers	600	D+	D
Range managers	150	A	A
Recreation specialists	5,900	B+	B
Registered nurses	71,000	A	B
Religious workers	3,400	D	D
Sales representatives:			
Manufacturers	9,500	F	B
Real estate	28,500	D+	D
Retail trade	190,000	C	B
Securities	6,100	C+	C
Wholesale trade	30,000	C	C

Occupation	Average Annual Job Opening	Growth Trends	Competitive Prospects
Scientists:			
Agricultural	450	F	D
Atmospheric	225	D	D
Biological	1,900	C	C
Life	10,700	C	C
Life and physical	110	B	B
Marine	120	D+	D
Political	600	C	D
Social	450	C	C
Social workers	30,500	B+	B
Sociologists	750	C	C
Speech pathologists	3,700	A+	B
Statisticians	1,250	C+	B
Surveyors	3,600	A	A
Teachers:			
College	14,000	F	F
Secondary	37,600	F	F
Elementary	94,000	F	F
Therapists:			
Occupational	1,000	A	B
Physical	2,400	A+	A
Respiratory	6,800	A+	A
Urban planners	700	B	B
Veterinarians	1,450	C+	B
Wholesale trade sales	30,000	C	C
Writers: Technical	1,150	D+	C

Figure 2-6. Cont.

SALARIES

One important element of career information is salary data. No one makes a career decision on the basis of one variable alone but in every ranking of variables important to career choice, salary consistently ranks somewhere within the top ten factors. The relative ranking of the factors important to career choice varies considerably based upon an individual's personal value system.

In approaching the career exploration process, most people want to collect salary information. Finding hard, accurate information often requires perseverance and digging. Salary averages change rapidly. Some people tend to resist releasing personal salary information even though the aggregation of personnel data guarantees anonymity. People also tend to lie a little because they want others to feel that they (or their profession) are better off than others.

Authors of books seldom print salary averages because such information rapidly makes obsolete the publication and reduces potential sales or requires more frequent revision which reduces profits. As a result, the best source of salary information for college graduates is the college placement office, want ads, and newspaper articles.

Offers to Graduating Students

Graduating students tend to be honest and cooperative in sharing salary information with each other. Salaries usually fall within a narrow range. This lack of wide dispersion between offers reduces the need for secrecy which results because someone is embarrassed over a low offer or someone is on a dollar ego trip.

Graduates should turn in every offer received to their college placement office with the position title and monthly base dollar amount. Nearly every placement office participates in a national salary survey with the national College Placement Council, a nonprofit professional association. The college sends a one-page survey form that gives the degree level, major subject, industry, and base salary for every offer to the Council for tabulating. Student names are not sent! Many employers—through the local placement office—also provide salary data to include in the survey.

In January, March, and July, the College Placement Council prepares a multipage report which is sent to participating colleges. Information is then released to the news media in the local area by the college placement office.

Salary information released by the local placement office and the national Council provides the most valid source of salary statistics. Data are released by degree level and subject field. Averages, medians, ranges, and number of offers give one a wealth of new information to include in the career decision-making process. Useful guideline statistics provided in Figure 2-7 are based on information from the latest "Salary Survey."

Salary levels are based on three major factors: employer policy, supply and demand, and the candidate's credentials. Some employers view themselves as salary leaders and pay top dollar to attract supposedly the top graduates each year. Many employers hire many of the top candidates, place them in very competitive situations, watch the cream come to the top, and keep the best and lay off the rest.

AVERAGE MONTHLY SALARIES
BY CURRICULUM AND DEGREE LEVEL

	Bachelor Degree			Master Degree		
	Low	High	Median	Low	High	Median
Accounting	900	1,200	1,100	1,100	1,500	1,300
Business	800	1,200	1,000	1,000	1,700	1,400
Engineering	1,200	1,500	1,300	1,350	1,700	1,500
Chemistry	900	1,300	1,100	1,100	1,550	1,350
Computer Science	900	1,200	1,100	1,200	1,600	1,400
Humanities	500	1,000	800	800	1,200	1,000
Social Science	600	1,000	900	900	1,250	1,050

Based on national averages of 1978. Ranges based on the middle 80%. Starting rates generally increase 5% to 7% annually.

Figure 2-7.

```
┌─────────────────────────────────────────┐
│                                         │
│           EMPLOYERS' SALARY             │
│          LEVEL DETERMINANTS             │
│                                         │
│         Employment Policies             │
│         Supply/Demand Situation         │
│         Applicant Qualifications        │
│                                         │
└─────────────────────────────────────────┘
```

Figure 2-8.

```
┌─────────────────────────────────────────┐
│                                         │
│          CANDIDATE RELATED              │
│           SALARY FACTORS                │
│                                         │
│         Degree Level                    │
│         Academic Major                  │
│         Work Experience                 │
│         Academic Record                 │
│         Leadership Activities           │
│                                         │
└─────────────────────────────────────────┘
```

Figure 2-9.

Other employers prefer to come in at the salary midpoint and hire candidates from a broad spectrum of backgrounds. Many hire exactly the number of new employees needed and provide a development program designed to build the qualifications of those less productive. Still other employers focus on hiring the "diamond in the rough" who through perseverance and hard work will outperform the "barn-burners" at the top of the class.

There are as many different employment and salary policies as employers. The array of different approaches cannot be defined here.

The second major factor influencing salary levels is the local supply and demand situation. Salaries vary by parts of the country, economic conditions in certain sectors, environmental setting (urban/rural/suburban) and cost of living considerations. Salary schedules often center on the local factors and new employees must be merged into the schedule with a minimum of disruption of existing staff relationships.

Finally, a job candidate's qualifications and competitiveness enters into the determination. A job applicant's worth may be dictated by considerations outside the immediate control of the employer. The most influencing factors as given in Figure 2-9 determine the exact offer amount.

The majority of employers start with a base dollar amount depending on degree level and academic major. The base amount results from the employment policies and the supply/demand situation. The amount may be above or below national averages. Amounts often referred to as "adders" make up the final figure. The adder amounts supposedly correlate with a judgmental opinion of what it might take to hire the candidate, yet be consistent with existing internal salaries being paid to current employees. Few employers offer salaries that exceed the salaries of current employees who are doing similar work.

The most directly related adder is previous full- or part-time work experience, preferably former job related experience. Some employers reward superior academic experience while others use it only as a selection factor. Most employers recognize other factors such as leadership activities, related interests, maturity, personality, and communication skills as part of the salary determination or selection factor. In essence, all of these add up to competitive variables that distinguish job applicants from each other.

Salary Differences

National standards for starting pay in the private sector, state and local government, and education do not exist. Even the published federal government salary schedule contains elements of flexibility. Because of changing economic variables and individual competitiveness, free market forces determine rates of pay.

Commonly held attitudes pertaining to certain sectors suggest that rates of pay contain some consistency. Many attitudes (such as "retailing is long hours and low pay," "teaching pays poorly but is secure," "oil companies pay exorbitant salaries," "public employment means low pay," etc.) represent no truth. Generalizations offer no valid career information!

A low paying sector or industry often contains several employers that represent salary leaders. The reason some industries pay more than others is often because they recruit more technical personnel where the demand exceeds the supply. Other industries may have most of their facilities where there are high rates of unemployment and hence the industry pays less than the average.

Figure 2-10 shows the differences in a five-year period of time of indexed salary rates for hiring of Master in Business Administration majors. If this figure was reranked on the basis of hiring engineers, the ranking of low paying to high paying industries would change significantly. Yet, assuming a $10,000 salary, pay rates by industry vary only from

INDUSTRY SALARY INDEX
(100 = CURRENT SALARY AVERAGE)

Industry (Salary rank order)	Salary Index	Percent Hired
All Industries	100	100%
Consulting	107	2
Packaging Materials	106	4
Motor Vehicles	105	7
Oil	105	6
Chemicals	104	8
Banking	103	18
Machinery	102	4
Food Processing	102	3
Metals	101	2
Rubber Goods	100	1
Electronics	99	6
Aerospace	99	1
Accounting	97	28
Construction	95	2
Utilities	93	3
Merchandising	92	5

Source: Association of MBA Executives. Based upon a five-year average of MBA hiring.

Figure 2-10.

$9,200 to $10,700, hardly enough differential to sway an important career decision from one group to another.

Trends

Salary rates change over time. In the past ten years starting salary increases kept slightly ahead of the rate of inflation. In the survey shown in Figure 2-11, starting rates for accounting increased faster than starting rates in engineering. In the next ten years, starting rates for engineers will probably increase faster than any other field but no one knows for sure.

Based on past trends, evidence suggests that starting salary rates will increase by an annually compounded rate of 4% to 6% per year or near the current rate of inflation. To avoid paying experienced people the same or less than starting college graduates, employers will probably increase current employees' salaries in the 5% to 8% range.

Dr. Frank Endicott (formerly Placement Director, Northwestern University) conducts studies each year on employer hiring practices. The 1977 Endicott Report showed that employees who started with a firm ten years ago and who were still with the same employer increased their salary far in excess of current starting rates. For example, Figure 2-12 shows that starting rates for general business increased by 55% in ten years while the individual who started the same ten years ago increased his/her salary by 165%.

This does not imply that everyone can expect to more than double starting salary in the next ten years. Given certain assumptions about inflation, job performance, job mobility, etc., a doubling of starting salary in ten years is not an unreasonable goal. It can be done by getting a 7% salary increase every year.

Salary Caveats

Collecting salary information produces pitfalls. In the final analysis, salary relates directly to job performance! Employers hire college graduates to work and produce results: Profits in the private sector and quality service in the public sector.

College graduates get paid higher salaries for their "potential" performance rather than their ac-

STARTING SALARY TRENDS
(MONTHLY SALARIES—10 YEAR PERIOD)

	Bachelor			Master		
	1966	1976	Percent	1966	1976	Percent
Engineering	$676	$1,165	72%	$797	$1,353	70%
Accounting	594	1,033	74%	700	1,224	75%
Business	548	852	55%	733	1,352	84%
Liberal Arts	536	835	56%	NA	NA	

Source: Endicott Report, 1977.

Figure 2-11.

AVERAGE MONTHLY SALARY
COLLEGE HIRES WITH EXPERIENCE

Field	5 Years Experience (Class of '71)	Percent Increase	10 Years Experience (Class of '66)	Percent Increase
Engineering	$1,658	87%	$2,045	157%
Accounting	1,720	101	2,275	225
Sales Management	1,637	124	1,939	163
General Business	1,448	106	1,942	165

Source: Endicott Report, 1977. Includes only graduates who started with the surveyed firm and are still with the same firm and includes private sector firms only.

Figure 2-12.

tual performance the first year on the job. The starting salary often exceeds that paid to many long-term blue-collar workers whose immediate contribution may add more to the bottom line in the short run.

Besides the investment in salary and benefits, employers often lay out an additional $30,000-$40,000 investment in facilities, equipment, trainers, and supporting staff for every new college hire. The moment the "potential" for adding more than cost to the bottom line disappears, the prudent employer faces a termination decision.

College graduates live on "potential" for six to eighteen months. At some short-term point, contribution must exceed cost. The feedback comes in the form of the performance review and superior feedback. In general, the higher the initial salary, the sooner the employer expects a reasonable contribution to the organization. In some assignments, particularly those above entry level, employers may expect an immediate contribution.

Quoting median salaries tends to demoralize individuals in the half of the class who by definition received offers below the median. The median becomes the base (or low range) in people's mind. Everyone cannot be in the top half. Few job candidates admit to themselves that they are in the lower half.

As offers come in at the appropriate amount, graduates may believe they have been treated unfairly. A tendency exists to "bad mouth" the organization which reinforces to colleagues and others that the candidate is, in fact, bottom half material. The interactions further create a ego defacing syndrome.

All of the concern about salary washes out quickly once on a job. Salary advancement depends upon performance. Within one year, no one remembers or cares about starting rates. Starting rates get determined from a rather inexact method. Any inequities usually disappear as rates are set on more objective criteria.

Some employers make paying lower than average salaries part of employment philosophy. The philosophy is to leave a wider latitude for rewarding top producers on the job. Except for sales type assignments, the upward limit on salary progression is based on salaries of employees hired in the past one or two years in the same job classification. Many employers prefer to leave as wide a gap between the two groups as possible to provide motivation for the new hires to excel.

Unlike nonprofessional jobs and jobs requiring significant experience, salary level is not usually a negotiable item at the entry level for college graduates. Salary desires may be asked before an offer is extended. Once the offer is extended, it is the rare employer that dickers. The overwhelming majority of ethical employers will withdraw an offer if there is a hint of salary negotiation. Firms occasionally raise all extended offers if the marketplace changes and they have a number of offers outstanding. Even those who accept usually share in that type of across-the-board increase.

The best way to keep on top of the salary issue is to discuss the situation with a placement professional. If every student turns in offers (low and high) to the placement office, fair and equitable guidance is possible. Where a given employer is way out of line, the placement office may be in a position to communicate circumstances to the employer on behalf of everyone, not just a single student.

Starting salary should not be a major concern.

In the final analysis, the decision to join a given organization is usually based on factors more related to advancement potential, people, location, honesty, life-style, etc. Even in the short run, differences of $50-$100 per month between employers impact little upon later career success which is the most important variable.

SUMMARY

The supply of college graduates is one variable that should be factored into the career decision, but it should not be disproportionately weighted. The job gap of about 100,000 graduates annually is likely to result in more underemployment than unemployment. Unfortunately, the mix in college majors does not mesh smoothly with job requirements. Future growth in employment is likely to come from service industries.

Salary information is another variable to consider in career decision making, but it rarely is *the* major factor in career choice. Salary averages vary widely by supply/demand, policy, degree level, and academic major. Salaries tend to grow slightly faster than inflation but depend solely upon job performance in the long run. Starting rates are based more on potential performance than actual contribution of the job to the organization. The best source of information is the college placement office.

3

EXPLORING CAREERS:
Environments — Structure — Positions

A problem facing graduating college students is the stereotyped image of work environments, organizational structure, and various career positions. Stereotypes may be false. The only way to determine the truth is to actively investigate each career option before deciding on a given course of action.

Few people have enough time to explore all possible avenues of career choice. The objective of this chapter is to bring together many of the variables that need to be explored. This can be accomplished by clustering a variety of related career fields based upon common elements in the work setting. The key points relate to the employment sector, the structure of the organization, and the entry-level assignments found in most jobs.

This chapter takes a superficial look at a limited number of career choices that must be made. The thrust is to spark an understanding of a broad context of work. The goal is to generate interest in exploring in much more depth given career options and to destroy inaccurate stereotype images of some fields where employment prospects appear bright. The entry-level positions covered represent the majority of positions normally open to college graduates.

EMPLOYMENT ENVIRONMENTS

"Who can I work for with a major in . . . ?" is one of the most frequently asked questions by stu-

dents of college placement officers. There is not enough time in anyone's life to explore all of the possibilities.

An overlay of the "world of work" reveals four major work settings: government, education, private business, and the professions. Within these work settings, there are major categories of occupations commonly referred to as white-collar, blue-collar, and service workers. Employment in government, education, and private business contains workers from each category including the professions although most professionals are in private practice.

College educated people may fall into any one of the four work settings. Within these occupational categories, college graduates most frequently work in white-collar jobs as managers, administrators, technical staff, professional sales, or in a profession.

WORK ENVIRONMENTS

Education
Government
Not-for-profit
Business

Figure 3-1.

Education

The primary sources of employment in education focus mainly on elementary, secondary, and higher education although related components include preschool, vocational education, special education, proprietary schools, etc. Most of the available jobs involve teaching, counseling, or administration but educational institutions hire a few people each year with special technical skills such as engineering, accounting, audiovisual, etc.

Very few employment sectors in education forecast any significant growth in hiring of fresh college graduates. Because of high turnover and some retirements, several thousands of job openings will develop, but the competition for each job is fierce as laid-off teachers, women returning to careers from being housewives, and current graduates vie for these jobs.

A tough job challenge should never deter one from entering a chosen profession. One should, however, recognize the competitive situation in order to best prepare superior credentials and aggressively hit the job market.

Not all areas in education deserve the depressed rating given the field in general. Dr. L. Patrick Sheetz, Michigan State University Placement Services, regularly researches the outlook for elementary and secondary teachers by teaching field. Writing in

a recent issue of *Graduate* magazine, Dr. Sheetz gave the assessment of the current situation shown in Figure 3-3. It is also advisable to put two or more of these teaching specialities together whenever academically possible. Consult the local educational placement office for the most current outlook.

Positions in elementary and secondary teaching almost always require a teaching certificate. More opportunities are available in intercity locations than in suburban schools. The doctorate is rapidly becoming a requirement in higher education and with the glut of doctorates in many fields, even the community colleges and small colleges can command a terminally degreed person. Although a doctorate is not currently required in many administrative assignments, the trend leans toward that direction for the future.

Government

Government employs over 17 million people in federal agencies, state governments, counties, cities, and municipalities. Governments hire graduates for nearly every occupational group although the exact job title may vary slightly. The federal government gets the most press coverage yet employs only 2.8 million while state governments employ 4 million and local governments over 8 million.

As a greater percentage of federal money returns to local governments, employment locally increases and stabilizes at the federal level. Unfortunately state and local governments employment hiring systems are not as standardized as the stabilized federal government which makes finding a job a bit more difficult.

Federal

Federal employment practices may be characterized: high competition for jobs; low attrition of current employees; internal attention to upward mobil-

---

POSITIONS IN EDUCATION

Teacher
Counselor
Administrator
Other

Figure 3-2.

RELATIVE DEMAND CATEGORIES
FOR ELEMENTARY AND SECONDARY TEACHERS

Positions Exceed Supply Greatly

Counseling (M.S. plus 3 years)
Diagnostician (Doctorate)
Industrial Arts
Learning Disabilities (M.S.)
School Social Worker (M.S.)
Vocal Music

Positions Exceed Supply

Agricultural Education
Business Education
Chemistry
Data Processing
Safety Education
Distributive Education
Driver Education
Earth Science
Journalism
Librarian
Mentally Handicapped
Physical Science
Physics
Reading Instruction
Swimming Coaching
Visually Handicapped
Wrestling Coaching

Positions Equal Supply

Art
Basketball Coaching
Emotionally Disturbed
Football Coaching
Home Economics
Instrumental Music
Mathematics
Physically Handicapped
Spanish

Supply Exceeds Positions

Baseball Coaching
Child Development
German
Golf Coaching
Men's Physical Education
Speech Correction
Tennis Coaching
Track Coaching
Women's Physical Education

Supply Exceeds Positions Greatly

Biology
Conservation
Economics
Elementary Education
English
French
Geography
Government
Health
History
Latin
Political Science
Psychology
Russian
Social Studies
Sociology
Speech
Theatre

Source: Michigan State University Placement Services, Dr. L. Patrick Sheets, *Graduate,* 1977.

Figure 3-3.

ity programs; and reductions in budget for hiring new staff additions. The translation means to start job campaigns early and get informed about positions available and application procedures.

Most college graduates enter under the "General Schedule (GS) Classification" in professional, scien-tific, administrative, or support personnel. Fourteen percent of all federal white-collar workers are in Washington, D.C. Only 2% work overseas. The average annual salary in 1976 for all white collar employees was $15,152. Professional salaries averaged $21,845 and administrative positions, $20,005.

College-level Entry

Two standard methods permit a recent college graduate entry into federal service: (1) the "Professional and Administrative Career Examination" (PACE) and (2) position "Announcements." Chances of employment depend upon how well an applicant compares with others in experience and education, the geographical location in which the candidate will consider employment, and the minimum grade or salary level. Candidates frequently eliminate themselves from consideration by restricting location and/or salary level on the application form.

The PACE examination is a standardized test for inexperienced college graduates with nontechnical degrees. PACE tests a series of ability areas (verbal, mathematical, judgmental, aptitude, etc.) and refers candidates on the basis of their scores to agencies listing vacancies which utilize the various ability categories.

Appointments from the "PACE Register" are made at the GS-5 and GS-7 levels, mostly at the lower level. Competition is intense (in 1976, 220,000 tested; 114,000 passed; 9,300 hired).

Occupations requiring a technical degree or specialized background are filled by individual "Announcements" and do not require the PACE exam. Some announcements require a written test more related to the job. Applicants are evaluated on the basis of education, experience, and ability to reflect their credentials clearly and accurately on the application form. Appointments are usually at the GS-5 or GS-7 level. Figure 3-5 gives the positions normally covered by the Announcement process.

Federal General Schedule Salary scales change annually. The rates are set to be competitive with comparable level jobs in private industry.

The Civil Service Commission operates a system of federal job information centers located in most major cities. These centers provide current information about employment opportunities, open announcements, testing, and application centers.

Certain federal agencies work outside the Civil Service Commission and manage separate hiring systems. These government and quasi agencies must be contacted directly. Figure 3-6 gives a partial listing of some of the more active hiring groups.

The PACE exam is given only a few times each year, and applicants receive results in about six weeks. Applicants must attend to deadline statements. Referral of candidates is done according to the "rule of three" which means that the top three persons on the register are referred to an agency with openings. After getting the scores applicants may "shop around" contacting agencies in which a certain interest exists. This searching technique is useful only if scores are in the 90-100 range.

Candidates must complete several application type forms. Complete these legibly and with great care and detail because answers are weighted in terms of the requirements for particular positions. Give much detail about extracurricular activities, volunteer work, part-time experiences, and complete descriptions of all full-time work. Successful candidates

---

FEDERAL EMPLOYMENT POSITIONS COVERED BY PACE

Administrative Trainee	Food and Drug Inspector	Personnel Specialist
Alcohol Tax Inspector	Geographer	Psychologists
Archivist	Historian	Public Information
Budget Analyst	Housing Intern	Realty Assistant
Claims Examiner	Intelligence Analyst	Revenue Officer
Community Planner	Investigator	Social Insurance
Contract Negotiator	Loan Examiner	Sociologist
Customs Specialists	Management Analyst	Statistical Assistant
Customs Inspector	Management Intern	Supply Specialist
Customs Technical Aid	Manpower Specialist	Tax Technician
Computer Programmer	Marketing Specialist	Writer and Editor
Economist	Museum Curator	
Financial Examiner	Park Ranger	

Figure 3-4.

FEDERAL EMPLOYMENT POSITIONS
COVERED BY ANNOUNCEMENTS

Accountant	Forester	Occupational Therapist
Aerospace Technologist	Geodesist	Patent Examiner
Air Traffic Controller	Geophysicist	Pharmacist
Animal Husbandman	Hospital Administrator	Physicist
Architect	Hydrologist	Pest Controller
Astronomer	Illustrator	Plant Scientist
Attorney	Internal Revenue Agent	Prison Administrator
Bacteriologist	Landscape Architect	Range Conservationist
Biologist	Librarian	Refuge Manager
Cartographer	Manual Arts Therapist	Social Worker
Chemist	Mathematician	Soil Conservationist
Dietitian	Medical Record Librarian	Special Agent
Education Officer	Metallurgist	Speech Pathologist
Engineer	Meteorologist	Teacher
Entomologist	Microbiologist	Therapist
Equipment Specialist	Nurse	Urban Planner
Estate Tax Examiner	Oceanographer	Veterinarian

Figure 3-5.

INDEPENDENT GOVERNMENT ORGANIZATIONS

Energy Research and Development Administration
Board of Governors of the Federal Reserve System
Central Intelligence Agency
Federal Bureau of Investigation
Foreign Service of the U.S.
International Monetary Fund
Judicial Branch of Government
Legislative Branch of Government
National Science Foundation
National Security Agency
Organization of American States
Tennessee Valley Authority
United Nations Secretariat
U.S. Mission to the U.N.
U.S. Nuclear Regulatory Commission
U.S. Postal Service
World Bank and IFC

Figure 3-6.

normally are geographically flexible. Patience is an important virtue. Start early.

State Employment

The size and scope of government operations vary considerably from state to state. States differ as to the process by which they hire new employees. Most states have personnel offices, but the functions are not always the same; some certify and recommend candidates to agencies; some directly hire for agencies; and some provide a central application and candidate repository service.

```
┌──────────────────────────────────────┐
│      STATE EMPLOYMENT FUNCTIONS       │
│                                        │
│           Conservation                 │
│           Criminal Justice             │
│           Education Programs           │
│           Elections                    │
│           Employment Services          │
│           Financial Operations         │
│           Health Services              │
│           Highway Operations           │
│           Law Enforcement              │
│           Legislative Liaison          │
│           Mental Health                │
│           Parks and Recreation         │
│           Prison Operations            │
│           Social Welfare               │
│           Transportation Systems       │
│           Unemployment Services        │
└──────────────────────────────────────┘
```

Figure 3-7.

```
┌──────────────────────────────────────┐
│      LOCAL GOVERNMENT SERVICES        │
│                                        │
│           Tax Assessment               │
│           Tax Collection               │
│           Elections                    │
│           Courts                       │
│           Law Enforcement              │
│           Urban Planning               │
│           Sanitation                   │
│           Health                       │
│           Social Work                  │
│           Welfare                      │
│           Roads and Streets            │
│           Parks and Recreation         │
│           Fire Protection              │
│           Public Records               │
│           Financial Services           │
└──────────────────────────────────────┘
```

Figure 3-8.

There is no consistency by states in employment in the utilization of testing, position classification systems, publicizing of open positions, use of patronage, and in college recruitment. Each state personnel office must be contacted directly. States obviously hire college graduates for similar roles as the federal government, but the applicant has a maze of fifty states to contact in order just to learn the rules of the game. Some states have residency requirements.

Local Government

Local governments (counties, cities, towns) offer employment opportunities in a variety of fields. Total employment in local government dwarfs both federal and state employment numbers combined. Although many governments have excellent merit or civil service systems, many have nothing and yet hire hundreds of people. It is common for individual agencies to do their own hiring, even at the managerial and professional level. Patronage and residency requirements often form barriers to the employment search.

Locating vacancies can be an expensive and complex process. The best advice is to visit each local jurisdiction and talk with the person responsible for hiring in each agency.

Quasi-private/Government

A few organizations which employ college graduates do not lend themselves to the government or private organization classification scheme. Most are not-for-profit corporations. They include hospitals, museums, symphony orchestras, art galleries, professional associations, labor organizations, consumer unions, industry trade groups, lobby and special interest groups, foundations, trusts, convention centers, auxiliary enterprises of educational institutions, etc.

For the entry-level assignment for the recent college graduate, the number of job possibilities do not represent large numbers. These organizations need qualified people. They need accountants, public relations specialists, marketers, engineers, negotiators, coordinators, etc. Unfortunately, there is no organized employment market so each unit must be contacted independently.

Private Business

By overwhelming margins, the largest employment sector for college graduates is the private organization. Business firms vary in size from the mom and pop grocery store to large multinational corporations. The free enterprise system permits doctors, lawyers, inventors, writers, store managers, distributors, manufacturers, farmers, etc., to set up a corporation for the purpose of generating profits and taking the risk of potential loss. All countries of the world do not share in this concept or accept the freedom of action principles. The free enterprise system generates more opportunities for young people than all other forms of employment combined.

A major goal of many college graduates is to eventually own and operate an entity they can claim as their own. The business might be a one-person private consulting firm, a ten-employee retail operation, or a multi-employee manufacturing corporation. Few graduates have the experience or financial resources to attempt a business of their own immediately after college. Most graduates look to the larger corporations to offer the foothold needed to get a start in their career.

Every business has a cadre of professional, technical, and managerial personnel who guide the organization. Most—not all—come from college educated backgrounds. That cadre is being replaced by a new generation of college trained managerial professionals and new cadres develop as new industries and firms create new products and/or services. Today's college graduates represent the leadership for tomorrow in these organizations.

Thousands of corporations in scores of industries dot the landscape of the United States. The industries represented include newspaper publishing, broadcasting, health, pharmaceuticals, banks, retail stores, restaurants, hotels, manufacturing firms, mining natural resources, etc. There are literally thousands of potential employers of college graduates. To visualize the myriad of possible industry groups, refer to Figure 3-9, which lists over 100 private industry groups.

Within each industry group, several hundreds of employers offer jobs to college graduates. Within each firm, many jobs with descriptive work titles exist. Each employee has a job title. For the college graduate, a basic set of position titles describe opportunities available. Employers often reserve a number of entry-level assignments for college graduates which are used as training positions for upward level assignments.

MANAGEMENT STRUCTURE

Every organization (including government agencies, hospitals, law firms, associations, small and large businesses) operates within some type of management structure. A management structure avoids chaos and defines relationships between functions (and people doing those functions). Invariably, when two or more people get together, formal and informal relationships develop. After a time, the relationships are translated into a hierarchical structure and leadership roles emerge.

Most organizations organize around basic functions or job duties that need to be accomplished. A grouping of all of the tasks needed to be done usually centers on three major functions: (1) create the product/service; (2) finance the product/service; (3) distribute the product/service. In business terminology, the three areas represent the manufacturing (buying or service), accounting/finance, and marketing/sales functions. Regardless of the institution, counterparts more than likely exist.

One of the first steps in career exploration is to determine where one fits best. Where do the job candidate's qualifications make the most significant contribution?

Management Substructures

As organizations reach a certain number of employees, the span of control for administering the three basic functions becomes less manageable. Maintaining the function concept, most organizations attempt to break down into smaller subunits. The breakdown may be by product, geographical location, type of service offered, or any other logical category.

There may be many managers/administrators within each function, and each function will have a manager. The functional managers report to the unit

PRIVATE INDUSTRY GROUPS

Advertising	Conglomerate	Investment Firms	Rail. Equip. Mfg.
Aerospace	Consulting	Labor	Real Estate
Agriculture	Copper	Lead and Zinc	REIT
Agri-Business	Cosmetics	Leasing	Recreation
Agri-Equipment Mfg.	Distilling	Life Insurance	Restaurant
Air Transport	Drug Mfg.	Machinery	Retail-Special
Aluminum	Drug Store	Machine Tool	Retail Chains
Apparel	Education	Magazine	Retail Dept. Store
Associations	Electric Utility	Maritime	School Supplies
Auto-Mfg.	Elec. Equip. Mfg.	Meat Packing	Securities
Auto-Parts	Electronics	Metals	Shoe
Auto-Service	Entertainment	Metal Fabricating	Silver
Auto-Sales	Fastener	Mining	Soft Drink
Baking	Finance	Mobile Home	Steel
Banking	Food Processing	Natural Gas	Sugar
Beverage	Food Distribution	Newspaper	Telecommunications
Brewing	Glass	Office Equipment	Textile
Broadcasting	Gold	Packaging	Tire and Rubber
Bus Transport	Grocery	Paper	Tobacco
Bldg. Materials	Health Care	Personal Service	Toiletries
Casualty Insurance	Health Insurance	Petroleum	Toys
Clerical	Home Building	Precision Instrument	Transportation
Coal	Hospital	Printing	Travel Service
Communications	Hotel	Public Accounting	Trucking
Computers	Household Products	Public Utility	
Construction	Industrial Service	Publishing	
Container	Insurance	Railroad	

Figure 3-9.

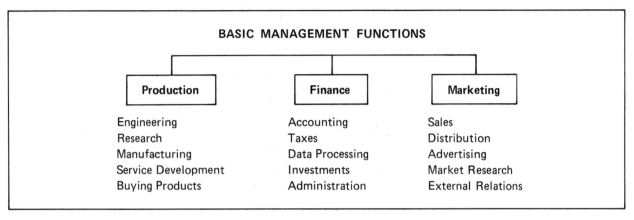

BASIC MANAGEMENT FUNCTIONS

Production	Finance	Marketing
Engineering	Accounting	Sales
Research	Taxes	Distribution
Manufacturing	Data Processing	Advertising
Service Development	Investments	Market Research
Buying Products	Administration	External Relations

Figure 3-10.

manager. A rule of thumb is that the span of control of any one manager is seven people. (It might be much greater where a person is managing a large production system.) Assuming that each function has seven major departments with managers and each manager has seven employers, it is easy to see that this one small subunit already has over fifty employees. This pyramiding concept is integral to most large organizations in government, education, or business.

To illustrate the complexity of organization structure, take a look at the top layer of management of a multinational corporation. The firm operates on seven continents and in 70 countries. Each country manager reports to a continent manager who reports to a vice-president. Each country is divided into seven zones. The firm manufactures 200 different products in 20 basic product groups. For each product, there is a production facility, financial managers, and a marketing system in each country. Clearly the complexity of the interrelationships between people in various locations is enormous.

No graduate could follow this maze for even one major organization. Recognizing this, most large organizations create entry-level assignments specifically designed for college graduates. The position's function is to attract high caliber people and to provide training. The training relates as much to learning the organization's structure, system, and philosophy as it does to learning a given job. Following the functional organization chart given in Figure 3-11 permits one to obtain a relative view of organizational life.

The Management Process

The term "managing" means an action oriented process of planning, organizing, motivating, and controlling an operation, system, or group of people. The managing process occurs in every basic phase of

any organization including accounting, marketing, manufacturing, engineering, research, and even among professionals such as doctors, dentists, nurses, etc. Managing occurs at "low" levels as well as "high" levels in the organizational structure. Managing involves policy determination, decision making, responsibility assumption, and supervision of people and systems.

The "manager" is the backbone of every organization. The manager designs, conducts, teaches, coordinates, and implements the managing process. The term "management" (administration) gets thrown around with little understanding of its true meaning.

When does one become a manager? Obviously, few (if any) people start their career as a manager. It takes time to gain the necessary experience which is essential to managing and supervising. There are various levels of management (junior, middle, top) in each specific function at each location. The entry-level assignment, usually related to a functional field, is the first rung of the management ladder.

Progression into various levels of management takes time which varies sharply between organizations and individuals. Some employers offer fast track, sink or swim, approaches while others prefer a planned development program. Some employers prefer to rotate personnel frequently between various job functions, geographical locations, product lines, etc., to gain a wide exposure to people, organizational philosophy, and cross training in a variety of functional fields. Others prefer a strict upward progression in a given functional field.

Upward Mobility

The candidate's ability to learn also impacts upon the time frame of upward mobility into management. Some people learn faster than others. Some

BUSINESS ORGANIZATION CHART

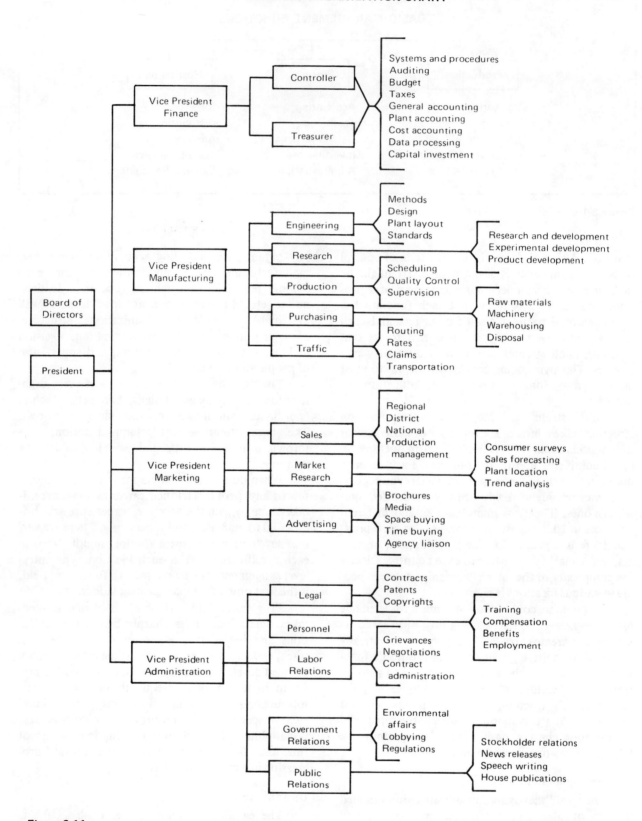

Figure 3-11.

fail—employment is terminated or the firm paints a picture on the wall. The automatic promotion system in school systems based on annual increments disappears. Promotion comes only after superior performance. Promotions can come in three months or take three years.

Because of some demographic changes in the United States population, upward mobility as a group is not likely to be as rapid as it was for past generations. The low birth rate of the depression and war years (1930-45) permitted that generation to fly into leadership roles. This generation moved into top management rapidly. The middle management position voids were subsequently filled by the postwar baby generation. Because of the relatively ages of young middle and top management today and the lack of major economic growth, one could predict a lot of musical chairs movement within the lower and middle management ranks within the next decade.

Not all individuals aspire to management responsibilities. A high percentage of college graduates fall into the ranks of management later, but this is not necessary. Managers tend to be the highest paid individuals in business, government, and education, but many organizations build in a comparable reward structure for high technology, research, and professional personnel.

CAREER POSITIONS

The employer's purpose in identifying certain positions as entry-level assignments for college graduates is to provide technical and managerial talent to run the organization in the long term. Few college graduates start at the top. The age-old tradition is to start at the bottom and work up. The college degree does not alter that fundamental concept. Often the entry-level assignment is not the rock bottom, but an intermediate step between blue-collar and white-collar, neither fish nor fowl.

Employers hire college graduates for potential, not necessarily immediately productive results. Most want productive results quickly, but the basic thrust is to develop long-term managers, professionals, or technical experts to run the firm. Some make it and some don't.

Figure 3-12 gives a definition of entry-level assignments and a broader statement of the motives and purpose of using such positions. No guarantees for advancement are usually given. Upward mobility is based on merit. Some employers hire more employees than needed because a certain level of failure is expected. Many nonperformers never get promoted and either get terminated, leave, or remain on low level assignments.

The entry-level concept works well for most organizations. Exact job titles used vary depending upon the size and type of organization. A few candidates never realize that they have been routed through an entry-level assignment.

Most assignments begin in one of the three basic functional areas of an organization:

1. Distributing (marketing/sales)
2. Creating or purchasing (manufacturing/engineering)
3. Financing (accounting/systems)

Depending upon the job sector and industry, some employers design a specific management trainee position which is used as a feeder into more responsible positions. Because of the college graduate's lack of interest in serving in a nonproductive "trainee" role, most employers have abandoned the

ENTRY-LEVEL ASSIGNMENTS

Definition

The entry-level assignment is a vehicle designed to introduce, smooth, and hasten the transition from an academic environment to an employment environment. The assignments are not lifelong commitments, oriented to pigeonhole people in the organization, but they do serve to provide career direction with an initial thrust. They often open multiple career paths unavailable to inexperienced people.

Purpose

Whether a training program or one of the more common direct placement assignments, employers use the entry-level assignments:

To introduce the many people with whom the new employee must work, both inside and outside the organization.

To expose the typical problems encountered by employers in the organization and field.

To provide an environment becoming immediately productive and making a positive contribution to the organization's goals.

To enable the new employee to begin applying and using skills as soon as possible.

To test and challenge the new employee with hard work.

To assist in determining the optional career path within the organization.

To evaluate potential.

The entry-level assignment is a mechanism which employers use to introduce and smooth the entrance into the organization. The entry-level assignments are not positions where they want people to stay indefinitely.

Figure 3-12.

management trainee approach. Those still using the "trainee" concept usually slot entrants into a functional field immediately after training.

Career Paths

Based on recent job openings sent to college placement offices, the most frequently referenced titles appear in Figure 3-13. The list is not all-inclusive but represents about 80% of available entry-level job titles used by business, government, and education employers. The title may change slightly depending upon job sector or industry, but the assignments change little in actual job content.

The entry-level assignment may have no relationship to later assignments but usually there is a tie between initial duties and upward movement. Most organizations tend to move people through a variety of assignments yet a common thread often seems apparent. This common thread represents the underlying career path of an individual. In most successful careers, detours from the primary career path provide a broadening experience. The detours may last several years.

Many organizations hire "career development specialists" whose role is to assist in the internal placement and career planning of employees. These individuals are in-house career consultants who assist employees in realistic career pathing within the organization. The career consultant (usually a high level executive with several years of personnel and development experience in the organization) assists in decisions to move employees laterally for additional experience, upward for promotion, to development programs for training, or job counsel for out-placement with another organization.

TYPICAL ENTRY-LEVEL JOB TITLES

Accountant	Inspector
Actuarial	Intern
Adjuster	Internal Auditor
Administrative Assistant	Investment Analyst
Advertising Assistant	Labor Relations Assistant
Agent	Laboratory Assistant
Analyst	Lawyer
Appraiser	Management Trainee
Assistant Buyer	Manufacturing Trainee
Assistant Director	Market Researcher
Assistant Manager	Marketing Assistant
Assistant to	Marketing Trainee
Auditor	MBA Consultant
Bank Examiner	Officer
Budget Analyst	Personnel Assistant
Business Manager Assistant	Programmer
Claims Representative	Purchasing Assistant
Copy Writer	Sales Engineer
Cost Accountant	Sales Representative
Counselor	Scientist
Credit Analyst	Social Worker
Distribution Analyst	Specialist
Economist	Statistician
Editor	Supervisor
Engineer	Systems Analyst
Executive Secretary	Tax Accountant
Expediter	Teacher
Financial Analyst	Therapist
Foreman	Writer

Figure 3-13.

Some areas of an organization serve as an entry-level point better than others. Entry within an organization normally does not imply a long-term commitment to the area. On the other hand, employers like to see young people who map out a career plan because that planning process demands the same type of objective analysis used in making most decisions. The analogy follows that if the person can plan ahead for their career, they have the basic abilities necessary in planning for the organization's success.

History teaches that movement within organizations for highly successful managers crosses many functional lines. Most often a successful career path is functionally centered. For example, the vice-president of finance usually started in finance but may have worked several years in both the marketing/sales and production/engineering functions during the rise to top management.

Most employers at the college entry-level assignment want to hear a candidate express strong interest in the functional field. Without the strong initial interest, success in the functional job may not develop. A statement like "I want to start in engineering but move into finance later" does not show sufficient interest in engineering to permit one to succeed.

Employers cannot guarantee upward mobility. Promotions for the first five years almost always occur in the starting functional field. Superior performance, measured by several promotions, permits cross-functional exposures. Until the functional field is mastered, a cross-functional experience is probably not possible.

Good advice is to lay out a career path for five to ten years in a given functional field. After five to ten years begin to request reassignment and pick up night school classes in another field.

International Exposure

Top management level aspirants in the multinational organization need an exposure to international operations at some point in a career path. International experience is not a requirement for top management, but in some firms it is very helpful. The corporation is not the place to look for an immediate overseas assignment. Most corporations look internally for management talent that have five to fifteen years of domestic expertise in a functional field, such as accounting, finance, sales, marketing, manufacturing, engineering, etc. Americans are sent overseas to help solve a specific problem.

Most employers fill overseas positions with nationals. Preference is given to nationals educated in the United States and who wish to remain in or return to their home country. Employers experience fewer

political, social, and economic problems with this policy. Overseas affiliates do their own hiring which is not directed through the American headquarters.

The large multinational firms do send Americans overseas for short durations of six to twenty-four months to assist the host country with a given problem and to develop management and technical expertise. Americans wishing to gain some international business experience should first accept functional employment with a corporation that has large international operations. After exceptional career progress in a domestic functional assignment, a request to be transferred to the international division is more likely to be honored.

Career Profiles

A career profile is a resume or synopsis of a given career field. Profiles assist in identifying areas of interests but do not give a complete picture of the career positions being reviewed. It is imperative that a review of these brief sketches be followed with an in-depth analysis of a given field. Even if a person has studied for several years in a given field, it is not wise to assume that that is the most appropriate field for his/her career interests and to plunge into a job search.

Several career profiles follow. The brief description of the career field may be used as a guide in deciding which fields merit further investigation. The selected profiles provide a format to use in analyzing fields not listed which may closer relate to a more technical background.

Cross-functional Training

Read every profile, not only those with titles closest to interests and academic major. Reading each one takes only a few minutes. During the interview and placement decision point, it becomes critical to have a strong awareness of all functions in an organization. Certain organizations place emphasis on given functional areas. Top management often comes from those fields. That point should be recognized by individuals in all other fields in order for transfers and other related experiences to be achieved.

It is not always easy to obtain cross-functional training in today's organizations; however, long-term career success may depend on cross training. To move to other fields requires a high level of awareness and some feel for the jobs. People who become top level general managers will have at some point in their career developed cross training. Knowing the basics about several functional fields before leaving college helps in moving up in organizations.

One caveat. Not all employers adhere to the profile just as all graduates do not measure up to resume claims. The job interview and employment brochures provide the detail.

CAREER PROFILE: MARKETING REPRESENTATIVE*

Marketing Representative   Account Executive   Sales Representative
Manufacturing Representative   Security Sales   Marketing Consultant
Technical Sales Assistant   Sales Engineer   Service Representative

Description

Maintains contact with customers . . . takes orders . . . liaison between two
parties . . . plans requirements . . . forecasts sales . . . projects supply
and demand . . . researches markets . . . introduces new products . . . assists
with inventory and production control . . . arranges delivery dates and methods
. . . services clients' needs . . . settles complaints . . . trains new employees . . . develops new customers . . . checks on competitors' activities
. . . prepares sales reports . . . representative at trade meetings . . .
arranges, coordinates, and sets up trade shows . . . influences product or
service design and price . . . assists in preparation of promotional materials
. . . coordinates advertising . . . public relations . . . trains new employees.

To the customer, the marketing representative is the organization! At all levels,
the marketing representative is part of the management team as decisions must be
made in the field.

Requirements

Requires no specific degree level; hire bachelor, master's, and doctorates. All
academic majors considered. Training programs teach the organization's product/
service characteristics. Interest in helping others is essential. Excellent
speaking ability. Strong skill in report and promotional style of writing.
Knack for problem solving and decision making. Requires strong self-discipline
as often set own hours and work routine. Need not be flashy, extroverted
stereotype but needs an outgoing, mature, pleasant personality. Prior work
experience not required. Extracurricular activities very helpful. May need a
semi-technical background in science, computers, or engineering with some industrial firms.

Advancement

Managers are responsible for product planning, promotional design, advertising
strategy, and staff administration. Managers supervise other managers, clerical
personnel, market researchers, marketing staff assistants, and sales representatives. May control a large geographical area or single product line. Responsible for budget preparation, financial control, and sales production of significant dollar amounts. May sell to large accounts. Representatives begin to
assume management responsibilities after one to three years of experience.
About 30 per cent of top executives are from marketing backgrounds. Individuals
on management tracks often spend one to three years in staff assignments in
marketing research, product management, and advertising.

Training

Training program orients to product/service characteristics and specifications. Acquaints with organization policy and personnel practices. Provides exposure to internal resources. Introduces to key customers and important contact.

Programs vary in length from a few days to two years depending upon the product line, industry, and type of training. Most training involves classroom seminars, evening study for exams, and on-the-job training with an experienced manager.

Earnings

Earnings based on annual salary paid monthly . . . may include a new automobile and attractive expense account above a base salary . . . bonuses are common at end of year in some industries . . . earnings can be very substantial in very short period of time . . . commissions and other incentive plans possible after a few years of experience . . . quicker high level earnings more likely than in most other fields even though entry earnings may not be high . . . most sales jobs require some travel but not necessarily away from home . . . travel depends on the industry, type of product and geographical territory.

Representative Employers

IBM	Carnation	Upjohn	Mobil
Kodak	Procter and Gamble	Merrill Lynch	Dow
Xerox	General Mills	Metropolitan	Ford
Alcoa	Brunswick	Doubleday	Amax
Lilly	Quaker Oats	Burroughs	NCR

Comment

Nearly every industry and occupation group has a counterpart to the sales representative. Outlook is especially strong as many smaller employers upgrade positions. Until recently, a college degree has not been required but is now becoming more essential. Best sources of additional information: Occupational Outlook Handbook, local libraries, employment brochures of major firms, job descriptions in classifieds, etc. Sales is one of the best bets for liberal arts graduates hoping to make use of their communicative abilities. Sales is one of the highest paying fields and the experience is directly applicable for individuals wishing to someday own a business.

CAREER PROFILE: RETAIL TRAINEE*

Assistant Store Manager   Executive Development Program
Department Manager   Management Trainee
Assistant Buyer   Operations Assistant

Description

Supervises sales workers . . . sells merchandise on floor . . . handles complaints . . . provides customer service . . . orders merchandise . . . meets
with manufacturer's representatives . . . travels to buying markets . . . determines price of merchandise . . . assists in advertising and promotional plans
. . . analyzes market . . . prepares marketing and sales reports . . . manages
and controls daily cash receipts . . . supervises inventory audits . . . trains
sales workers . . . hires sales and clerical personnel . . . assists in advertising copy preparation . . . designs and supervises building of displays . . .
shops competitors . . . operates as an independent profit center.

Requirements

Requires no specific degree level but most hiring is at bachelor level. All
academic majors get consideration. Some exposure to sales and accounting is
helpful. The people oriented business nature requires gregarious personalities.
Must be able to talk well with customers. Cannot be timid or shy personality
type. Competitive spirit is essential. No full-time work experience is necessary but work in a retail related assignment, such as sales worker, cashier,
counter duty, etc., is helpful. Extracurricular activities are a sign of leadership and involvement. For department stores, an interest in fashion is helpful.
Requires evidence of good report and promotional writing style.

Advancement

Upper middle management jobs are as buyers and store managers . . . buyers are
responsible for entire products or product lines which may run into millions of
dollars. Performance is tied to success of selling everything purchased at a
non-sale price . . . store managers supervise many people and control profits
for large segments of the retail business at a given location . . . retail estab-
lishments are divided into several types of concerns: Department stores and
national chains including discount stores, supermarkets, fast food stores, and
specialty shops. The career path is slightly different for each operation as
follows:

>   Department Stores: (1) Trainee, (2) Assistant Buyer, (3) Sales
>   Manager, (4) Buyer/Department Manager, (5) Store Manager, (6) Mer-
>   chandise Manager, (7) General Merchandise Manager, (8) Vice
>   President.

Career Planning and Placement Today, C. Randall Powell. Copyright © 1974 by C. Randall Powell. Copyright © 1974, 1978 by Kendall/
Hunt Publishing Company.

Chain Stores: (1) Trainee, (2) Assistant Department Manager,
(3) Department Manager, (4) Operations Manager, (5) Assistant
Store Manager, (6) Store Manager, (7) District Manager,
(8) Buyer Home Office/Regional Manager, (9) Vice President.

Training

The time spent as a trainee varies from six to eighteen months depending upon
policy and candidate performance. It normally takes three to six years to
reach the buyer/store management level. Training begins with seminars but
quickly goes to on-the-job training supplemented with regular seminars. The
first performance review is usually in six months with annual increases
thereafter.

Earnings

Retailers have a reputation for starting with low pay and substantially rewarding the high performers with superior salaries. The reputation is not universally true. The large department stores and chains pay extremely competitive
salaries to attract top students. The smaller retailers are slightly below
average. Buyers and store managers earn in the $18,000 - $40,000 range depending upon performance, merchandise line, and gross sales. In several recent
salary surveys, successful retail executives rank near the top of the industry
wide pay scales.

Representative Employers

Penney's	K-Mart	May Co.	The Gap
Sears	Venture	Macy's	Kroger
Ward's	Korvettes	Lazarus	Burdine's
Dayton's	Lord & Taylor	Safeway	Neiman Marcus
Gimbel's	McDonald's	Famous Barr	The Limited

Comment

For graduates who enjoy meeting people but dislike calling on customers retailing is the answer. Responsibility and earnings come rapidly. It is especially
enticing to individuals with an entrepreneurial flair who may want to start
their own business after some experience and savings. Most retailers require
employees to work only 44 hours normally but during certain periods the hours
get longer. There is often pressure, some travel for buyers, and night and
weekend hours. The challenge and attractive pay tend to negate some of the
drawbacks. The business is fast paced and action oriented.

<u>CAREER PROFILE: ADVERTISING/BRAND ASSISTANT</u>*

Market Researcher	Product Manager Assistant	Copywriter
Account Executive	Market Analyst	Staff Assistant

Description

Many organizations use advertising agencies to promote products and services to potential customers. Most opportunities for college graduates are in agencies because very few organizations maintain a large in-house advertising department. Organizations prefer to pay agencies an allocated sum to generate the creative messages.

Structure

An agency is a group of specialists trained in various facets of marketing. The objective is to increase sales of the client. Consequently, employees work in a highly charged, competitive situation full of extreme pressure and excitement. Major departments include:

<u>Marketing Research</u>. Conduct surveys by telephone and canvassing. Design questionnaires. Analyze responses using sound statistical and computer techniques. Write reports for management decisions.

<u>Copywriting</u>. Compose verbal messages and edit copy.

<u>Art and Layout</u>. Produce pictures, graphics, and artwork. Often use free lance specialists as models, actors, technicians, etc.

<u>Telecommunications</u>. Produce sound effects, video, audio, sketches, scenes, etc. in producing messages for broadcast. Often contract with local stations for service.

<u>Print Production</u>. Plan and order plates for magazines, newspapers, and brochures. Experts in reproductive processes, such as print, photo engraving, electro-plating, typography, etc.

<u>Traffic</u>. Plan the flow and timing of copy, production, art, etc.

<u>Account Executive</u>. Serves as liason with the client. Works with creative personnel in idea design. Submits copy and reworks design with client.

Market Research/Product Management

Large corporations usually in consumer goods industries occasionally have small staffs in market research and product management. People in these marketing and advertising departments may have come from the sales force or have been recruited right out of college. Those from college are usually Master of Business Administration graduates with prior experience in sales.

Marketing Research. Collect, analyze, and interpret market data . . . data comes from calls, questionnaires, or sales records . . . prepares reports on sales forecasting, brand name selection, packaging design, plant locations, distribution channels, and advertising strategy . . . most jobs are promoted from within assignments . . . may recruit experts like statisticians, computers, psychologists, economists, etc. . . . need exceptional writing skills . . . demand not strong . . . entry is often from sales staff.

Product Management. Responsible for coordinating every facet of product . . . includes advertising, pricing, packaging, manu- facturing, distribution, legal concerns . . . career path is relatively flat: assistant to manager to group manager . . . prepares annual marketing plan with research, forecasts, sales, profits, and advertising strategy . . . requires strong analytical skills, decision-making forte, and strong writing capabilities . . . often spend time in sales before and after this assignment . . . more frequently seeking prior experienced MBA graduates.

Advertising. Write copy . . . design layout . . . drafts initial mock-ups . . . plan media-use percentages . . . allocate advertising budgets to agencies, magazines, TV, radio, brochures, etc. . . . develop sales presentations . . . design trade-show materials . . . often is a temporary staff assignment from the sales force . . . requires exposure to various types of media.

Comment

Most employers in agencies, market research, and product management do not recruit at many colleges. It is necessary to contact potential employers directly. In contacting agencies, graduates should use the Standard Directory of Advertising Agencies, which lists over 3,500 agencies. Local media occasionally hire college graduates with sales being a common entry job. While the job prospects are not good in these fields, for aggressive indiv- iduals with strong creative talents these fields offer unique advantages.

CAREER PROFILE: PRODUCTION/ENGINEERING*

Supervisor	Purchasing	Project Engineer	Logistical Control
Foreman	Materials Control	Process Engineer	Plant Engineer
Scheduler	Warehousing	Engineer	Product Planning
Quality Control	Inventory Control	Design Engineer	Methods Analyst
Distribution	Systems	Operations	Analyst

Description

Supervise production personnel . . . schedule work . . . review output quality
. . . process raw materials . . . arrange transportation . . . order materials
. . . analyze production processes . . . design production process . . .
select transportation carriers . . . route raw materials and finished goods
. . . manage warehouse . . . design control systems . . . analyze work methods
of workers . . . develop quality standards . . . improve efficiency of operations . . . conserve energy . . . design equipment . . . develop new products
. . . establish safety standards . . . test products . . . design environmental control systems . . . create, design and implement engineering projects
. . . operate complex equipment and facilities . . . prepare cost estimates
. . . create managerial control systems for cost reduction . . . buy production equipment . . . order raw materials.

Requirements

Bachelor degree in some phase of engineering is preferred but with the shortage
of engineers, employers often hire candidates with backgrounds in related fields,
such as industrial management, production, mathematics, physics, chemistry, and
other academic fields that require use of quantitative and analytic experiences.
A few non-technical candidates are hired in supervision, scheduling, warehousing,
purchasing, and other fields where the analytical thought process is not necessary. Some jobs require a strong people orientation while others are analytical
and are project centered. Some jobs require a specific background in a given
discipline of science or engineering.

Advancement

Entry-level assignments often start as part of a team project concerned with
some aspect or problem area in production or design. Upward movement is sometimes in a given professional field rather than into management because many
people in this field do not desire management responsibility. It is not uncommon for individuals to remain professional engineers throughout their career
and assume more complex projects as experience warrants. The management option
is to move into people supervision, systems or unit management, plant manager,
superintendent, etc. Long-term advancement moves people into divisional manufacturing heads, research and development managers, and corporate vice presidents.

Training

Much of the initial training is on-the-job since candidates usually come to work with a high level of technical competence. To maintain this high level of skill in a fast changing technology, many organizations operate in-house technical centers through which employers are rotated on a regular basis. The team oriented projects help one keep current as people learn from each other. There are frequent plant and corporate level seminars. Most firms pay the tuition of employees who want to continue their education on a part-time basis.

Earnings

Individuals going into the field command the highest pay of all college graduates. As long as the supply/demand trend continues to raise starting rates so rapidly, candidates within the firms will continue to enjoy large pay increases. Annual raises of 10 per cent are not uncommon for the top 25 per cent. Chief plant engineers and managers in middle management earn in the $25,000 - $50,000 range. Top managers earn salaries in excess of $50,000.

Representative Employers

U.S. Government	Exxon	Rockwell	Goodyear
Alcoa	Chrysler	Bendix	Boeing
Borg Warner	General Motors	Kaiser	Dupont
Eaton	Union Carbide	RCA	Arco
Quaker Oats	Inland Steel	Owens-Illinois	Eli Lilly

Comment

Young people entering this function will find top salaries, challenges, and long-term opportunity. All is not glory as dirt, noise, long hours, shift work, daily change, people problems, production foul-ups, etc. become integral parts of the everyday picture. Non-technical entrants need to begin early in their career to prepare themselves technically in order to compete for the higher level assignments. Top management in certain highly technical industries traditionally come from the engineering and manufacturing ranks.

CAREER PROFILE: ACCOUNTANT*

Industrial Accountant	Financial Analyst	Cost Accountant
Tax Accountant	Administrative Assistant	Internal Auditor

Duties

Compile business records . . . prepare financial reports . . . develop profit
and loss statements . . . analyze financial records . . . prepare budgets . . .
conduct internal audits to insure adherence to acceptable accounting standards
. . . prepare balance sheets . . . make financial decisions . . . prepare control procedures . . . create financial systems . . . format data for machine
processing . . . write financial and credit reports . . . prepares capital
investment plans . . . develops a financial plan . . . work with bankers in
financial needs.

Requirements

Usually requires a minimum of a bachelor degree with an accounting major. Job
candidates with 15 or more hours of accounting plus some credit hours in finance
are often accepted. Strong report writing skills are important. No experience
is necessary but preference is often given to individuals with an internship
or coop experience. MBA graduates without an accounting major often start as
financial analyst or as an assistant to a manager. These mid-level assignments
are designed to provide on-the-job training exposure to the accounting function
to compensate for lack of course work.

Advancement

The chief financial officer (CFO) is the top position. May be titled controller,
comptroller, treasurer, or vice president. Next level includes division controllers, plant controllers, chief accountants, financial analysts, assistants,
and departmental managers which represent middle management ranks. Departments
include:

Internal Auditing	Credit Analysis	Data Processing
Operating Budgeting	Cost Control	Systems and Procecures
Capital Budgeting	Financial Accounting	Programming
Treasury Staff	General Accounting	Tax Preparations

More and more promotions are made from within the ranks of current employees.
This is closing many doors for the young people who start work for a CPA firm
and later join an industrial firm. A few firms move MBA graduates into lower
middle management ranks which places them at a level similar to where BS
level employees with two years experience are.

Training

Many employers formalize the initial training to maximize the exposure to a wide variety of assignments. Training is usually on-the-job with an experienced person guiding daily learning. In-house training is frequently supplemented with outside seminars and home office programs. Many industrial employers urge employees to prepare for the "Certified Management Accountant" (CMA) certificate, which is the industrial equivalent of the CPA.

A rotating array of assignments appear to be the pattern with many employers. Most want employees to get exposed to all phases of the finance function. Unlike the public accountant's monotonous audit routine, the industrial accountant gets a wider variety of tasks. Promotions usually fall every two to five years. Promotions go more to individuals with strong writing and speaking abilities as managers more and more must explain their decisions in an articulate fashion.

Earnings

Entry-level earnings on the average exceed the average rates paid to college graduates. Performance reviews are conducted annually with earnings increments of two to three percent above the rate of inflation, plus substantial boosts as promoted. Promotions come every two to four years. Chief financial managers are among the highest paid executives in business and government. Many advance to the presidency in business.

Comment

Most initial jobs demand attention to detail . . . work is of a project-related nature . . . assignments vary considerably . . . travel demands increase as one moves up into the management hierarchy . . . auditors may travel constantly from location to location living on expense accounts . . . promote from within concept is growing . . . financial staff is close to the high level decision-makers . . . young people can gain much exposure to top management in a short time frame . . . many top cost-conscientious executives come from finance ranks.

Representative Employers

U.S. Government	RCA	Caterpillar
DuPont	3M	U.S. Steel
Goodyear	PPG	Cummins Engine
Blue Cross	NCR	Burroughs
Shell Oil	GE	Chrysler

CAREER PROFILE: PUBLIC ACCOUNTANT*

Description

Public accountants are independent practitioners who work on a fee basis for organizations needing financial records verified. Government regulations require many organizations to hire a third party to review financial records. The three major functions of public accountants are: (1) report the financial facts, (2) attest to their authenticity, and (3) advise clients of proposed plans of action.

Requirements

Most public accounting firms require 24 - 30 semester hours of accounting courses and a four-year college degree. Most seek graduates in the top 25 per cent of the graduating class and rarely drop standards below 3.2 on a 4.0 scale. CPA firms need the assurance that employees can later pass the rigorous national CPA examination. Public firms accept a smaller percentage of accounting graduates each year as the supply goes up and demand levels off.

Public firms turn down a high percentage of students in the top 25 per cent of their class. It takes more than grades. Employees constantly meet with clients so outgoing personalities and highly developed speaking skills are essential. There are many reports to write and public relations work with each client.

Advancement and Training

Staff "assistants" usually begin in the audit branch of the firm. Most firms have a tax and management service component which hire a few off campus, but more frequently move people internally. Only about 10 per cent of the individuals beginning as staff accountants reach the top partner level. The initial training period is aimed at orientation and preparation for passing the CPA examination. Supervisors regularly meet with new employees to review work assignments and offer professional assistance.

Typically the staff accountant is given one area of the audit (verification of cash balances, inventories, receivables, etc.) and asked to evaluate the client's control procedures and to verify the accuracy of the figures.

The second level is the "senior" accountant, who assumes responsibility for field assignments and for supervising several staff assistants. The promotion comes in two to four years after which much of the "dog work" is a thing of the past. The "senior" is rotated to a variety of jobs and assumes responsibility for small jobs. There are various levels of seniors. Employees stay at this level two to four years.

The third level is the "manager" who maintains direct contact with the client's problems, personnel, organization, and accounting methods. Managers assign seniors and assistants to jobs. The manager, with the partner, writes the "management letter" to the client suggesting ways to improve operations. Some firms have an intermediate level known as a "supervisor" before the manager stage. Most managers have five to eight years of experience before reaching this level and remain in the assignment four to eight years. Some plateaus exist at this level.

A partner bears the responsibility of management and takes part in decision making and policy formulation. Final responsibility for servicing clients rests with partners. Partners maintain and foster relationships with accounts and deal with questions regarding fees, services, and recent developments in the industry. There are also various levels of partners. It normally takes twelve to fourteen years to reach the partner stage.

Earnings

Superior initial earnings . . . $500 - $800 increment for passing all parts of CPA examination . . . increases of 2 - 4 per cent above current rates of inflation for partner track candidates . . . promotion raises are 10 - 15 per cent of base pay . . . assistants can earn overtime pay with some firms . . . overtime can equal 10 per cent of base pay over the year . . . at entry level, a graduate degree is worth about a 10 per cent premium . . . small regional firms may pay 15 - 25 per cent less than large national firms . . . the senior earns 50 - 70 per cent more than entry level . . . managers earn two to three times the earnings of assistants . . . partners earn in excess of $40,000 annually but must make a financial contribution to the firm's capital.

Comment

Less than 20 per cent of those who start with a public firm remain in ten years. Attrition due to flunk-outs and better opportunity is high. Some of the reasons given for the high turnover are the long hours at tax time, overnight travel, and tedious nature of auditing. As more and more employers adopt promote-from-within practices, the opportunity for the recycled CPA to join major firms in other than entry-level positions might be remote. The two to three years of work experience in public accounting before joining an industrial firm may not be the wave of the future; yet, the level of opportunity to learn and chance for advancement is hard to find in any other profession.

Representative Employers

Arthur Andersen	Haskins & Sells	Touche Ross
Arthur Young	Peat, Marwick & Mitchell	Alexander Grant
Coopers & Lybrand	Price Waterhouse	Hurdman & Cranstoun
Ernst & Ernst		

CAREER PROFILE: FINANCIAL INSTITUTIONS*

Money Center Banks   Savings and Loans   Insurance
Regional Banks   Credit Unions   Brokerage
Local Banks   Loan Companies   Real Estate

Description

Evaluate credit . . . invest funds . . . provide financial advice . . . make
decisions on installment, commercial, or real estate loans . . . appraise
property . . . conduct actuarial studies . . . evaluate risk . . . investment
planning . . . coordinate work flow . . . evaluate and design paper processing systems . . . manage people at all levels . . . sell services . . . public
relations . . . devise advertising strategy . . . conduct economic research
. . . forecast economy . . . draw up contracts . . . service contracts . . .
design forms . . . evaluate claims . . . process paperwork . . . buy and sell
stocks and bonds . . . analyze securities . . . provide customer contact and
service . . . prepare periodic reports . . . maintain records . . . customer
inquiries and complaints . . . develop budgets . . . implement cost control
procedures . . . train and recruit personnel.

Requirements

A bachelor degree in some phase of business administration is preferred, but
they often hire candidates without business backgrounds especially if candidates have taken some accounting and/or finance courses. Some money center
banks primarily recruit MBA degree holders. The paperflow is tremendous
so outstanding report writing skills are required. For jobs involving public
contact, a pleasing appearance and good speaking characteristics are essential.

Job Areas and Titles

Credit Analyst   Commercial Lending   Management Trainee
Branch Manager   Investment Analyst   Claims Adjuster
Operations Manager   Appraiser   Broker
Loan Officer   Credit Cards   Agent
Trust Administrator   Management Service   Actuary
Security Analyst   Underwriter   Auditor
Data Processing   Accounting   Programmer

Advancement and Training

Most financial institutions set aside several positions for entry-level positions. Training programs tend to rotate new salaried employees into a variety of different areas. A structured and planned on-the-job training with key personnel identified as top trainers is common. Some employers offer regular seminars and take home assignments but most simply encourage attendance at a local college and pay tuition for job-related courses. The typical career path is: (1) Trainee, (2) Assistant/Analyst, (3) Department/Branch Manager, (4) Junior Officer, (5) Officer, (6) Manager of a Major Division.

Earnings

Money center banks tend to be salary leaders, but most are located in large metropolitan areas. The large insurance firms and regional banks start employees at a competitive salary. Other financial institutions tend to start college graduates at salaries slightly less than the average but provide excellent benefits, working conditions, less pressure, and higher job security. Financial institutions have one of the highest benefit packages. Salaries of officers with large banks equal those paid in manufacturing firms. Salaries in smaller organizations often top out in the $50,000 - $75,000 range. Successful salespeople in insurance security sales and real estate often earn far in excess of what salaried employees earn.

Outlook

As the U.S. moves into more credit cards and a checkless society, more and more opportunities for graduates will emerge. Financial institutions may add to their professional staffs yet lower overall employment. Financial institutions are service oriented and highly competitive which keeps pressure on to develop new services for the public and thus hire college graduates to manage the functions.

Representative Employers

Bank of America	Mellon National	Metropolitan
Chase Manhattan	American Fletcher	Lincoln Life
Continental Illinois	Boatman's	Allstate
Republic National	Citicorp	Prudential
Merrill Lynch	Associates	State Farm

CAREER PROFILE: PERSONNEL/PUBLIC RELATIONS*

Personnel Assistant	Benefits	Public Relations
Labor Relations	Safety	Legislative Concerns
Training	Personnel Services	Copy writing
Compensation	Publications	Speech writing
Employment	Affirmative Action	Recruiting

Description

Directs personnel programs . . . administers policies . . . sets personnel objectives . . . interviews salaried and hourly candidates . . . refers qualified candidates to department managers . . . writes classified ads . . . travels to recruit people . . . develops recruiting itinerary . . . prepares manpower plan . . . canducts wage and salary surveys . . . maintains employment records . . . compiles statistics . . . devises complex pay structures . . . administers benefit programs . . . prepares payroll reports . . . knows government wage regulations . . . current or social security laws . . . handles employee grievances . . . participates in labor negotiations . . . writes speeches for executives . . . edits in-house publication . . . designs and gives orientation program to new employees . . . administers job classification system . . . writes job descriptions . . . assists in job performance evaluation . . . designs forms . . . sits in on government compliance reviews . . . assists in company lobby efforts.

Requirements

Requires a bachelor or master's degree . . . preference given to applicants with personnel training . . . complex government laws and regulations are creating ,a bureaucratic structure of specialists . . . still hire some generalists but trend is toward specialists where available . . . course work needed in industrial relations, labor relations, labor law, industrial psychology, sociology, personnel management, organizational behavior . . . public relations people need strong writing skills, attractive appearances, and outgoing personalities . . . public relations requires extremely strong writing abilities . . . background needed in journalism, communications, English, etc.

Basic Functions

Employment. Hiring of hourly workers . . . screening of salaried personnel . . . college recruiting coordination . . . writing classified ads . . . analyze jobs . . . prepare job descriptions . . . write job specifications . . . administer employment tests . . . conduct performance reviews . . . assist promotions, and terminations . . . coordinate action.

Career Planning and Placement Today, C. Randall Powell. Copyright © 1974 by C. Randall Powell. Copyright © 1974, 1978 by Kendall/ Hunt Publishing Company.

<u>Training</u>.   Orientation programs . . . seminar coordination . . . audio-visual
aids . . . human relations programs . . . company library . . . suggestions
systems . . . training manuals . . . tuition program administration.

<u>Compensation and Benefits</u>.   Develop wage scales . . . conduct wage surveys . . .
administer benefit program . . . comply with wage and hour laws . . . understand
social security regulations . . . administer vacation plans . . . design stock
option plans . . . design and administer pension plans consistent with laws . . .
administer company insurance plans . . . maintain employee records.

<u>Labor Relations</u>.   Expert on labor laws and history . . . contract negotiations
. . . grievance procedures . . . legal arbitration . . . contract administration
and interpretation.

<u>Public Relations</u>.   Provide information to newspapers and media . . . write
speeches . . . coordinate executives' engagements . . . write copy for company
publications . . . prepare handbooks and manuals . . . design layouts and
graphics . . . conduct attitude surveys . . . often come from a journalistic
background.

Advancement and Training

The entry-level job is usually as a personnel assistant or trainee. The next
move may be as an assistant department manager in one of the basic functions
from which functional managers are selected. Most firms rotate personnel
between functional fields but the increasing complexity of OSHA, ERISA, EEO,
ELSA, etc. may force more specialization. Some firms use personnel as a
12 - 30 month temporary rotational assignment for line managers. Most training is OJT supplemented by training seminars sponsored by professional
associations.

Outlook

The number of candidates needed annually is very low. The supply of candidates
greatly exceeds the demand; however, many candidates applying do not have the
necessary credentials. Candidates trained in either personnel or public relations have the best shot at available jobs. Because of the walk-in and write-in
applicant traffic, very few employers actively recruit candidates even when an
opening exists. Starting salaries are below average. Salary progression is
often slower than in other functional areas, but people in these fields do not
go into it for the money. Most really enjoy the type of work routine.

4

SEARCH STRATEGY:
Resumes — Letters — Contacts

By now some entry-level position targets have been established, and it is necessary to develop a strategy to implement these plans. There is a good way and a bad way to do almost anything. This chapter assumes possession of a general goal, up-coming graduation, and that some help is needed in how to go about finding employment. A step-by-step preparation for the job hunt is important because it leads to one of the most important lifetime decisions that probably ever will be made.

Half of the task of getting the right entry assignment is said to be being in the right place at the right time. To be sure, luck plays a role, but luck is made by those who begin the proper planning that will put them in the right place at the right time. The key to that task is communication! The basic communication tools are the resume, letters, and oral presentations by telephone or in person.

THE RESUME

A resume is an individually designed written summary of personal (address, age, interests, etc.), educational, and experience qualifications intended to demonstrate an applicant's fitness for a particular position or positions. It is a digest of qualifications for a job.

The resume should be structured to focus attention on qualifications and achievements and should demonstrate how they make a candidate attractive for the type of position being sought. A resume is sometimes also referred to as a vita, data sheet, interview form, etc.

Preparing the Resume

There is no one accepted way or format for preparing a resume. Unlike company application forms and the standardized college interview forms used by placement offices, the resume is given in a free format and can highlight assets while minimizing limitations. Standard forms force one to give all data requested regardless of how it bears on qualifications. For example, most forms request overall grades while the free form resume lets one omit low grades and highlight more recent ones if the latter grades are nore indicative of ability.

The resume *differs in principle* from standard forms. Application forms present basic facts about background in an organized scheme so that employers can rapidly screen on key factors and readily compare the qualifications of the various candidates competing for a given job opening. By contrast, the purpose of the resume is to introduce the prospect to the employer and hopefully help obtain an interview. Its purpose is not to get the job.

Almost no employers hire candidates based on their resumes. It is the job interview presentation that more often gets the firm job offer. The resume whets the employer's appetite to the extent of wanting to set up an interview. The resume is an essential tool in organizing a job campaign; but it should not be relied upon for anything other than opening a door or two.

Resume styles and formats vary considerably. Length is determined largely by work experience and leadership activities while in college. Resumes of recent college graduates almost never exceed one page in length; resumes of two pages might be appropriate for persons with more than one year of professional related work and/or military experience so that the jobs (duties and responsibilities) can be detailed. Even for persons with extensive experience, resumes of three or more pages are rarely effective. Remember that the purpose is to get an interview, not substitute for a more effective verbal presentation.

The sample resumes in this book offer ideas that may be useful to college graduates with varying levels of experience and campus activities. There have been some extremely innovative approaches to resume preparation especially by individuals applying for positions requiring unique creative skills such as in advertising.

Graphically, the resume should be easy to follow. Sentences may be incomplete. Employers may read resumes for hours each day so they search for key points; one that is concise and easy to follow stands a better chance of getting the individual concerned selected for an interview. Resumes should be reproduced through high quality processes such as photocopies and offset printing. Carbon copies should never be used. The yellow pages of the telephone directory provides a listing of copy service businesses.

Some experts recommend a passport size (2 1/2 × 3 inches) photograph for the resume. Individuals have used unique clusters of photographs in work related poses to draw the employer's attention. Some people use the resume as a gimmick to get a foot in the door. There are advantages for attracting attention, but there are also negatives related to such tactics. Think ideas through carefully.

The application photo has one very important purpose; if the interview is obtained, it is easier for the employer to recall the applicant later. If interviews with twenty college graduates are conducted each day by a recruiter, it becomes increasingly difficult to recall individual people based solely on a piece of paper with a set of facts. Most people find remembering a specific individual easier when shown a picture.

Pictures also present problems. Job discrimina-

tion is on the mind of many applicants today. A photograph may help the employer identify sex. The applicant could get screened out (or in) based on sex. This is not a strong argument for including or excluding a picture from the resume because most applicants can be identified as male or female based on first name, sorority, fraternity, and activities.

A photograph may also identify race. Again, this has pros and cons, depending on race and point of view. Race is much more difficult to identify from other facts on the resume, but experienced personnel representatives can identify minorities from rather obscure facts on the resume. There are also some legal ramifications of placing a photograph on a personal resume although there are probably no laws against it. Some states do, however, have laws against employers requesting a photograph.

Elements of the Resume

A really good resume must be *written by the individual.* Experienced personnel representatives can easily spot professionally prepared resumes, and often these are the first to be discarded because they are not a sincere reflection of the person. But make no mistake—a resume is a sales device and requires that a few hours be spent working on it. It must present a *POSITIVE* image.

By carefully positioning the most important assets first, with the most space devoted to them, positive elements are stressed. All activities (school, work, military, or extracurricular) must show major contributions. These assets and activities are used to present a positive appeal that indicates to the employer a hard worker, a doer, a people relater, and one who is energetic, ambitious, and a self-starter. Most resumes have eight major parts, each of which is discussed below and relate to each of the sample resumes shown.

Identification. Prominent on any resume is the home address and telephone number. For contact at work, it is permissible to include the business name and office telephone number, but this is often not done because it may not be desirable for a present employer to know other employment is being sought. It is necessary to include a permanent address (parents or relatives) because people move and employers may try to make contact a year or two later.

Personal Data. This includes marriage status, birth date, dependents, and occasionally any physical limitations. Personal data may appear at the top (after identification) or near the bottom.

Professional Objective. This is perhaps the most important part of the resume because the reviewer must know the type of job being sought before extending an invitation for the interview. Few college

graduates bent on professional careers are willing to present resumes which say, "Here are my qualifications, what do you have for me?" The company may be interested in someone for a job shoveling coal! Few employers interview without a job opening. An applicant's job interests must match the employer's openings before the applicant is invited to interview. This area on the resume can cause more trouble than any other if not handled properly.

The objective should be broad enough to cover any suitable employment. This decision should not be left up to employers because they are not likely to make the decision for the applicant. For multiple interests, one should consider preparing a resume for each area. In most cases one can easily determine which resume to give to which employer. At all costs, it is critical to avoid giving the employer the idea that such an important career decision cannot or has not been made or that the specific position desired is not important. In most professional jobs, the individual is asking to be considered as a decision maker for the firm and could come across as a nondecisive person.

Some sample professional objectives are given in Figure 4-10. It should be remembered that the remaining portion of the resume is designed to support why the applicant would make a most attractive candidate for the specific entry position being sought. Education, work experience, background, and perhaps references should consistently support interest in the specific opening being sought. For example, a resume designed to interest a banker in an applicant's qualifications for a banking career would likely be substantially different from a resume formatted to reflect an interest in an assistant buying job with a progressive retailer. Conceivably, an individual could be interested in both, so for best results, the two resumes should be structured differently.

One way some graduates attempt to solve the problem of making the objective broad enough to in-

terest a wide array of specific employers and specific enough to give an element of sound career direction is to omit the topic from the resume and include it in the letter of application. The letter is discussed in the next section. The disadvantage of this approach is that the resume and letter seldom stay together. The letter may accompany the resume when seeking an appointment, but it is often necessary to supply an additional resume when taking the interview. The resume is the tool designed to represent the individual and is often shared with others in the organization and may get separated from other supporting comments about job interests. In addition, this approach does not permit the objective to reaffirm qualifications listed in other parts of the resume. The other parts should continually reinforce and support interests stated at the top of the resume.

Education. The highest degree level should come first. It is not necessary to include high school but all colleges should be identified. However, if some items in a high school background show high honors, leadership traits, and generally reinforce the career objective, then that pertinent data should be included. In addition to the degree earned fron each school, the applicant should indicate dates attended, graduation date, major subject, honors (Phi Beta Kappa, Dean's List, Cum Laude, Beta Gamma Sigma, etc.) and all other information that will enhance the individual's qualifications for the career objective.

Applicants having high grade point averages should include them; if not, then they can comment about grades in their major subjects, more recent grades, steady grade improvement, or that work encompassed a certain number of hours per week each semester. For certain types of employment possibilities, applicants should list grades in selected courses that relate directly to the job. for example, for a job in personnel, grades and courses such as industrial relations, organizational behavior, collective bar-

```
┌─────────────────────┐
│ Sample Resume       │
│ Graduating Senior   │
│ No Experience       │
└─────────────────────┘
```

Resume of Joe E. Doe

Present Address   Home Address (Parents)   Personal
University Quadrangle   James J. Doe   Born 2/17/XX
Apartment 3-X   123 Wells Avenue   5'11", 170 lbs.
Bloomington, IN 47401   Indianapolis, IN 46800   Excellent health
812-337-5555   317-333-4444

Career   Sales Representative. Wish to begin my career in an industrial firm where
Objective   the products to be marketed are of a semi-technical nature. Eventually hope
                to become a marketing vice president or other high-level executive in a firm
                with strong marketing orientation in an industrial goods product line.

Education   Indiana University School of Business (8/XX to 6/XX)
                B.S. degree in Business Administration, June 197X. Have been on Dean's List
                two semesters out of the last three semesters...Overall grade average of 3.1...
                Took elective courses in cost accounting, data processing, sales management,
                marketing strategy, retailing, and advertising.

                Purdue University College of Engineering (8/XX to 6/XX)
                Started college with the idea of becoming a mechanical engineer...Took
                several hours in chemistry, physics, calculus, and engineering principles
                while at Purdue...Overall grade point average was a B+...Because interests
                were found to be more people oriented, transferred to Indiana University.

Campus   Pledged and initiated into SAE social fraternity at Purdue...Actively
Activities   participated in basketball and baseball intramural sports...Played these
                sports as a varsity letterman in high school...Reporter for the Exponent
                (campus newspaper) my sophomore year.

                Active member of the I.U. Student Foundation both years at IU...Active in
                campus politics (ran for senior class president but defeated)...Public
                relations chairman of Promise Party, junior year...Part-time disc jockey
                on Quad radio system...Captain of baseball and basketball intramural teams.

Work   Part-time Janitor, Indiana University (8/XX to 6/XX)
Experience   Worked ten hours each week to provide spending money while at college...
                Superior was pleased with my industry...In spite of the low status and pay,
                learned much about people relations in this task...Supervised the "swing"
                people who came into my area of the building.

                General Laborer, Indiana State Highway Department. (Last four summers)
                Worked 50 to 70 hours per week...Cut grass, patched ruts, dug ditches, drove
                tractor, shoveled rock, put up signs, flagman, etc...Earned and saved enough
                money to pay tuition for two semesters.

Background   Brought up in Indianapolis...have three brothers...father works for U.S.
                Post Office...lettered in two sports (basketball and baseball) in high school.

References   Dr. C. R. Powell   Mr. D. Blair   Mr. James Jackson
                Prof. of Bus. Admin.   Asst. Basketball Coach   Dir., Halls of Residence
                Indiana University   Indiana University   Indiana University
                Bloomington, IN 47401 Bloomington, IN 47401   Bloomington, IN 47401

December, 19XX
```

**Figure 4-1.**
```

RESUME OF SUSAN L. CHASE

Present Address
1430 Capitol Street
Apartment 115
Green Bay, WI 54303
(414) 192-7082

Home Address (Parents)
William H. Chase
4354 West Huffman Avenue
South Bend, IN 46614
(219)391-2842

Business Address
HCB Stores Inc.
Greenville, Ohio 52000
(815) 336-9999
(Mark PERSONAL on Inquiries)

OBJECTIVE

To continue my career in personnel as a personnel assistant with additional exposure to recruiting, training and development, benefit administration, and compensation administration. Eventually wish to become a personnel manager.

EDUCATION

INDIANA UNIVERSITY SCHOOL OF BUSINESS (8/XX to 5/XX)
B.S. degree in Personnel and Industrial Relations, May, 197X. Have an overall grade average of 3.1. Have taken elective courses in commercial law, typing, and shorthand. Have 20 hours of personnel courses including labor relations, salary administration, personnel measurement, and organizational behavior.

Pledged and initiated into Kappa Delta social sorority; served as assistant treasurer and treasurer. Inducted into Alpha Lambda Delta, freshman women's honorary. Member of card section and attended all basketball games. Served on the Alumni and Public Relations committee of I.U. Student Foundation.

WORK EXPERIENCE

ASSISTANT PERSONNEL MANAGER, HCB STORES, INC.
Involved with recruiting, selling costs, budgets, and to some extent training and development for the Greenville stores. Currently, I am working on an orientation manual for new employees. (2/2/XX to present)

MANAGEMENT TRAINING PROGRAM, HCB STORES, INC.
While at the Madison East store, exposed to sportswear, juniors, china and gifts, and trim the home departments. Gained basic knowledge in merchandising techniques, price changes, sales techniques, management of sales-people, schedules, and reviews. (6/15/XX to 2/2/XX)

TERMINAL OPERATOR, UNITED STATES AUTO CLUB, MOTORING DIVISION
Served as a terminal operator and general clerk during the summer (5/15/XX to 8/15/XX)

SECRETARY, SOUTH BEND COMMUNITY SCHOOL CORPORATION
Worked in the transportation and purchasing departments during the summer. (5/15/XX to 8/15/XX)

REFERENCES

Dr. C. R. Smith
Industrial Relations
School of Business
Indiana University
Bloomington, IN 47401
(812) 337-1000

Dr. T. James Crawford
Chairman
School of Business
Indiana University
Bloomington, IN 47401
(812) 337-1000

Ms. Joanne Bendall
Home Economics Coord.
Community School Corp.
635 South Main Street
South Bend, IN 46601
(217) 296-3300

Figure 4-2.

Sample Resume
Graduating Senior
No experience

Resume of Sally Jones

Campus Address (until 6/1/XX)
Pigskin Apartments
Apt. 2-B
Bloomington, Indiana 47401
812-226-1111

Married - will relocate
Husband is an engineer

Home Address
Care of James K. Jones
123 Front Street
Chicago, Illinois 60601
606-333-5555

5'2" - 110 pounds
Born May 12, 1954

CAREER OBJECTIVE

Sales Representative. Objective: To start career with a firm that markets office products (or similar products/services) . . . My work has exposed me to most equipment from typewriters to computers . . . Relate well to office management personnel because understand their problems . . . Enjoy the personal discipline and autonomy of sales . . . Desire a high technology firm with training designed to offer management potential.

EDUCATION

Indiana University, College of Arts and Sciences, Bloomington, Indiana
Will earn the A.B. degree in Economics, June, 19XX . . . Hold a 3.8 overall grade average and have earned all A's in Economics . . . Minor field is in journalism . . . Anticipate election to Phi Beta Kappa.

University of Illinois, Circle Campus, Chicago, Illinois
Began college as a part-time student here while I worked as a full-time sales clerk in a local clothing store . . . Transferred to I.U. with 30 credits after one year . . . Earned a GPA of 3.0.

CAMPUS ACTIVITIES

Captain of the women's varsity tennis team for two years. Member and officer in Kappa Delta Sorority (social) . . . Night editor in junior year of the Indiana Daily Student campus newspaper . . . Historian on Mortor Board, a senior women's honorary . . . Selected as advisor to President Ryan my senior year . . . Active in the I.U. Student Foundation program, particularly the "Little 500," a bicycle race whose proceeds provide scholarships.

WORK EXPERIENCE

John H. Jones, Attorney at Law, 8/XX to present
Part-time secretary . . . Handle filing, occasionally take dictation, transcribe tape recordings of proceedings, type contracts and other legal instruments, and more recently, training another person.

Jane's College Shop, Junior Sports Wear, 8/XX to 6/XX
Sales Clerk, part-time . . . Worked approximately 10 to 15 hours per week servicing customers . . . Frequently assisted the manager-owner in designing advertisements and promotional displays . . . During my last three months before semester end, often supervised and scheduled other clerks when the owner was out of town.

Treasure Place Gift Shop, Every summer since high school
Various assignments . . . Mother owns this unique gift shop in a tourist area just north of Chicago . . . Specialize in items from the Scandinavian countries . . . Have done everything from sweeping out the storeroom daily to helping select merchandise at the semi-annual trade shows . . . Show customers around, handle some of the daily accounting, develop displays, manage part-time salespeople, do all correspondence, etc.

PERSONAL

Married in my senior year . . . Husband is a Purdue engineering graduate who works for a consulting firm . . . Father is a sales engineer in Chicago . . . Have traveled extensively in Europe and lived one year during high school in Japan . . . Can operate most office equipment including copiers, calculators, microfilm equipment, and computers . . . Type 70 wpm . . . Know some computer programming . . . Speak Spanish and Japanese.

References upon request . . . resume prepared October 19XX.

Figure 4-3.

**BUSINESS PLACEMENT
INDIANA UNIVERSITY
Bloomington Campus**

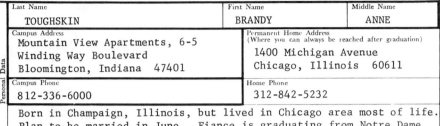

Personal Data

Last Name	First Name	Middle Name
TOUGHSKIN	BRANDY	ANNE

Campus Address	Permanent Home Address (Where you can always be reached after graduation)
Mountain View Apartments, 6-5 Winding Way Boulevard Bloomington, Indiana 47401	1400 Michigan Avenue Chicago, Illinois 60611

Campus Phone	Home Phone
812-336-6000	312-842-5232

Born in Champaign, Illinois, but lived in Chicago area most of life. Plan to be married in June. Fiance is graduating from Notre Dame and will be attending law school at Northwestern. His father is a lawyer in Evanston so we expect to stay in Chicago area.

Type of Work

Entry Level Assignment Desired	Career Objectives
Retail Development Program Assistant Buyer Department Manager (soft goods)	Begin career with a department store offering a training program that exposes one to operations, advertising, display, supervision, sales training, and buying and opportunity for advancement into merchandising.

College Information

Name and Location of Colleges Attended	Dates From	To	Degree Earned	Graduation Date	Major	Grade Pt. Av.	Grade Basis	Class Rank Quartile
INDIANA UNIVERSITY Coll. of Arts and Sciences	8/XX	5/XX	A.B.	5/6/XX	Home Economics	2.8	A=4.0	II
Northwestern University Evanston, Illinois	8/XX	7/XX	--	--	Spanish	2.2	A=5.0	IV

Hold a 3.2 GPA in my major. Have taken courses in marketing, sales management, retailing, and accounting. Familiar with data processing. Specialized in textiles.

College Honors and Honorary Societies, Professional Societies, Extra-curricular Activities, and/or Other Information

Delta Gamma Social Sorority: President, 19XX; Treasurer, 19XX; Rush Chairperson, 19XX.
Vice-President of Panhellenic: Responsible for changing the rush system for all sororities.
Night Editor, Indiana Daily Student: Editor and reporter for two years.
Union Board Trustee: Assisted in managing a very large Student Union operation.
Hobbies: Singing and acting in college theatre; play reserve on women's basketball team.

Employment Information

College Expenses Earned	How Earned
%	

Work and/or Military Experience (Names and Addresses of Employers)	Title and/or Description of Work	Hours Per Week	Dates Employed From	To
Marshall Field & Co. Chicago, Illinois	College Board. Assisted buyers in selection of new fall fashion merchandise in juniors	40	Su, 19XX	Su, 19XX
Sears and Roebuck Evanston, Illinois	Sales Clerk. Worked as vacation relief which gave a wide view of all parts of retailing	40	Su, since jr. yr. in high school	

As my academic load and schedule permitted, worked part-time for Block's College Shop, a young women's specialty store. Worked from sophomore year until present when needed as a sales clerk. Had a sundry of duties including sales, security, stocking, cash control, gift wrapping, minor supervision, etc.

(Attach Addendum if Desired)

General Information

References: (Names and Addresses—Preferably Two Faculty and Two Business)

Prof. C. U. Around Chairperson Home Economics Indiana University Bloomington, IN 47401	Prof. I. M. Smart Marketing Department School of Business Indiana University Bloomington, IN 47401	Mr. J. L. Business Vice President Marshall Field & Co. 100 Michigan Avenue Chicago, IL 60601	Mr. L. Eagle, J.D. Attorney at Law Eagle, Eagle & Eagle 101 Michigan Avenue Evanston, IL 66014

I certify that the above information is accurate. I authorize the Indiana University Business Placement Office to use this information for employment and related purposes. Unless otherwise advised in writing, Business Placement may refer this resume and attachments to potential employers and graduate schools.

Date Signed	Social Security No.	Signature
September 10, 19XX	303 - 55 - 2241	*Brandy Ann Toughskin*

B84—4-75

COLLEGE INTERVIEW RESUME

Figure 4-4.

| Sample Resume |
| Graduating Senior |
| Limited Experience |

BILL SWILL
1632 Holloway Avenue
Ft. Wayne, Indiana 47000
314-866-1000

PROFESSIONAL OBJECTIVE	Retail Store Sales Manager or Buyer. Ultimate goal--Manager of major retail outlet for large national chain or Merchandise Manager for department store.
EDUCATION 19XX to 19XX	BS, 19XX, INDIANA UNIVERSITY Major: Marketing Minor: Mass Communication Special emphasis on retail sales and merchandising; considerable work in accounting and data processing.
EXPERIENCE 19XX to 19XX	HARTMANS, INC., Fort Wayne, Indiana Assistant Manager. In charge of all advertising and copy layout for this large department store. Work closely with all buyers in planning sales campaigns. Materially assist manager in working out modernization plans for basement floor. Have taken two trips to Dallas, Texas to assist in selection of men's suits and shoes.
19XX to 19XX	J. C. WHITE & COMPANY, South Bend, Indiana Retail Shoe Sales. Started as clerk in Elkhart store. After six months, moved to South Bend outlet as Assistant Manager. Responsible for all display work, newspaper advertising, and sales promotion. The store has an annual volume of $290,000.00.
SUMMER WORK	Earned 50% of total college expenses selling vacuum cleaners and cooking ware on commission for four summers.
MILITARY SERVICE	United States Army, 19XX to 19XX Communications Specialist. After graduation from college, enlisted in the Army. Spent most of the time in Europe working as a communications and personnel relations officer.
BACKGROUND	Brought up in Northern Indiana area. Active in community affairs such as Junior Achievement, Boy Scouts, and active alumnus of Indiana University. Member of a social fraternity. Wife is a Doctor's Aid in a local clinic. No children. Have traveled extensively throughout the Midwestern and Southern United States.
INTEREST	Primarily interested in hiking--outdoor activities and conservation societies, e.g. Sierra Club, Save the Redwood Foundation, Audubon Society, etc.
PERSONAL	Married 5'11" 170 Pounds Excellent health
REFERENCES	References will be furnished upon request.

Figure 4-5.

Sample Resume
Graduate Student

Resume of John E. Jones

<u>Present Address</u>   <u>Home Address</u>
123 Smith Road   R.R. 25, Box 25
Anytown, USA 96122   Anytown, USA 96211
812-444-5555   812-444-4444

                           5 feet 10 inches
Engaged   175 pounds
Born June 17, 195X   Excellent health

<u>Professional
Objective</u>

An immediate goal is employment on an accounting staff of a large industrial firm or public institution that will provide a wide exposure to different accounting problems. Eventually wish to become controller of a major organization.

<u>Education</u>

Sept., 19XX
to
June, 19XX

INDIANA UNIVERSITY GRADUATE SCHOOL OF BUSINESS
<u>Earned the Master of Business Administration degree in June, 19XX.</u> Major subject was finance and have taken a large number of courses in quantitative business analysis with the idea of developing a strong background in management information science. Earned a 4.0 in my major subject and held a 3.65 average overall. During the second year of the program, taught the basic accounting courses as a teaching assistant. Treasurer of the MBA Association that year. College expenses were financed by the assistantship and the G.I. Bill.

Sept., 19XX
to
June, 19XX

THE OHIO STATE UNIVERSITY COLLEGE OF ADMINISTRATIVE SCIENCE
<u>Earned the BS degree in June, 19XX, with a major in accounting.</u> Grades in the accounting field averaged 2.8. Overall GPA was 2.5 although earned a 3.5 my last two quarters. Took 35 semester hours of accounting courses. President of the Accounting Club during senior year. Pledged the Phi Psi social fraternity my freshman year and elected president my junior year. Played intramural basketball every year.

<u>Work
Experience</u>

Employed as a part-time sales clerk for about 10 hours per week every quarter while at OSU in the campus bookstore.

Summers

Worked summers while in undergraduate school as a welder in my uncle's tool and die shop. This position, plus my part-time work, paid for 75 percent of college expenses as an undergraduate.

Military

Sept., 19XX
to
June, 19XX

U.S. ARMY - Commissioned as a 2nd Lieutenant in September, 197X, after completing ROTC at OSU. Began active duty by attending Signal Corps at Ft. Gordon, and Ft. Monmouth, New Jersey. Served as a communications officer in Japan in 197X. Also spent one year in Europe. Currently 1st Lieutenant in the active reserves.

<u>Personal</u>

Born and reared in Gnaw Bone, Indiana. Youngest of nine children. Father was a local businessman and sheriff. Plan to marry in June following MBA graduation. Wife is also from southern Indiana and a graduate of IU. We prefer residing in a medium to small community.

<u>References</u>

Dr. Joe Smith	Dr. Curt Jones	Dr. James Monroe
Professor of Finance	Professor of Accounting	Vice President
Indiana University	Ohio State University	Gnaw Bone State Bank
Bloomington, IN	Columbus, OH	Gnaw Bone, IN

February, 19XX Date completed

Figure 4-6.

```
┌─────────────────────────┐
│ Sample Resume           │
│ Person with 4-8 years of│
│ Professional Experience │
└─────────────────────────┘
```

Resume of John W. Smith

Business Address
Controller's Staff
ABC Electronics
One Market Square
Indianapolis, IN 47000
317-444-4444

Home Address
1000 West Oak Street
Indianapolis, IN 46202
317-555-5555

OBJECTIVE: To become Controller, Treasurer, or V.P. Finance of a small to medium sized organization located in the Midwest.

EXPERIENCE:

19XX to Present

Assistant Controller, ABC Electronics Inc., Indianapolis
Corporation manufactures electronic components and has a sales volume of $60 million in three Midwestern plants.

Responsible for supervising the accounting functions including cost accounting, tax accounting, data processing, and budgeting. Duties involve supervision of cost analysis, inventory control, budget preparation, tax advising, etc. Principle projects involved:

- Established an effective system of job cost analysis that led to a major change in product pricing and an increased profit.
- Redesigned cash management system which greatly reduced need for short-term funds.
- Recommended major acquisitions program that led to merger with a compatible capital intensive company.

Promoted from Financial Analysis to Cost Accounting to Chief Accountant during my tenure.

19XX to 19XX

Manager, Jones and Company - CPA's, Louisville
A medium size regional firm with two national accounts, several local OTC firms, and many local organizations.

Started as a Junior Accountant on the audit staff and progressed to Manager. Duties involved audits, tax preparation, SEC registrations and systems design. Spent several months in the Management Services Department.

EDUCATION:

19XX to 19XX

MASTER OF BUSINESS ADMINISTRATION, INDIANA UNIVERSITY, Bloomington.
Course work was concentrated in finance and management. Earned a G.P.A. of 3.75 and was elected to Beta Gamma Sigma. Passed all parts of CPA examination before leaving. Completed degree in May, 19XX.

19XX to 19XX

BACHELOR OF SCIENCE, ACCOUNTING, UNIVERSITY OF NOTRE DAME, South Bend, IN
Completed 33 credit hours in accounting and 12 hours in finance.
Treasurer of Alpha Beta Delta Social Fraternity during my junior and senior year. Active in campus politics. Maintained a 3.1 G.P.A. overall.

PERSONAL Born November 11, 194X, in Jeffersonville, Indiana, where I played varsity basketball and track in high school. Married with two children. Wife works as a school teacher.

REFERENCES: Furnished on request. Please do not contact current employer without my permission.

Figure 4-7.

CHARLES DRINKWELL

Home: 304 Jones Street
        Nashville, Indiana 47644
        812-444-0000

Business: National Sales Manager
            John Beam, Inc.
            Gnaw Bone, Indiana   47744
            312-333-0000

OBJECTIVE
Sales Executive/Marketing Manager/V.P. Marketing

SALES PROMOTION

Devised and supervised sales promotion projects for large business firms and manufacturers, mostly in the manufacturing field. Originated newspaper, radio, and television advertising and coordinated sales promotion with public relations and sales management. Analyzed different markets and costs. Developed sales training manuals. As Sales Executive and Promotion Consultant, handled a great variety of accounts. Sales potentials in these firms varied from $50,000 to $3,000,000 per year. Was successful in raising the volume of sales in many of these firms 30 percent within the first year.

SALES MANAGEMENT

Hired and supervised sales staff on a local area, and national basis. Established branch offices throughout the United States and developed uniform systems of processing orders and sales records. Promoted new products as well as improving sales of old ones. Developed sales training program. Developed a catalog system involving inventory control to facilitate movement of different stock between branches.

MARKET RESEARCH

Devised and supervised market research projects to determine sales potentials, as well as need for advertising. Wrote detailed reports and recommendations describing each step in distribution, areas for development, and plans for sales improvement.

SALES

Retail and wholesale. Direct sales to consumer, jobbers, and manufacturers. Hard goods, small metals, and electrical appliances were sold.

ORDER CLERK

Received, processed, and expedited orders. Set up order control system which was adopted for all branches.

FIRMS

19XX to Present	John Beam, Inc.	National Sales Manager
	Nashville, Indiana	
19XX-19XX	Jack Allen Widgets Co.	Product Manager, Market Research
	Peru, Indiana	Staff, Sales Promotion Manager
19XX-19XX	Pfeiffer Bros. Electronics	Sales Manager, Sales Representative
	Uptown, Indiana	

EDUCATION

Indiana University, B.S. 1956; Major: Business Administration/Marketing

PERSONAL DATA

Birthdate, February 10, 1924. Married, four children. Excellent health.

Figure 4-8.

JERRY MANNEY
111 West Street
South Bend, IN 46298

Home: (219) 666-1111   Business: (219) 666-5544

Marital Status: Married   Health: Excellent
Dependents: One   Height: 5'10"
Birthdate: January 23, 194X   Weight: 165
Birthplace: South Bend, IN   Citizen: U.S.A.

OBJECTIVE

To utilize the skills developed in evaluation, planning and managing in order to increase profits and achieve special economic objectives. Goal is to seek a chief operating officer position with a major corporation.

EXPERIENCE

FINANCIAL: Responsible for Profit Planning, Budgeting, Cost Systems, Working Capital Management, and Cash Flow in Corporations ranging from less than $1,000,000 in assets to over $100,000,000 in assets. While fully conversant with sophisticated methods of capital budgeting and asset management, also experienced in working with line production personnel in this function.

SALES AND MARKETING: Responsible for individual Sales Territory, Product Management, Product Planning, Sales Budgeting, Sales Management, Group, Divisional, and Corporate Marketing Plans. This experience is primarily in industrial markets with corporations and units ranging from less than $100,000,000 annual volume to over $300,000,000 annual volume.

PRODUCTION: P/L Responsibility for Individual Products, Special Projects Cost Systems, Production Planning Systems, Asset Disposal, Capital Budgeting, Cost Reduction Budgeting, and Asset Justification.

ADMINISTRATION: Experienced in all phases of administration with special emphasis on systems and organizational planning. Fully conversant with the organizational problems encountered in both small business and large corporations. Successful administration of both line and staff groups leading to a very clear understanding of the mode of operation and objectives of each type of organization.

EMPLOYERS

New Fibers Incorporated (19XX-19XX)
    a. Area Sales Manager
    b. Manager Operations Analysis
Associate Corporation of America (19XX-19XX)
    Manager of Corporate Acquisitions, Business Analyst, and Forecasting
Packaging Corporation (19XX-19XX)
    a. Marketing Project Director for NOW Products
    b. Manager Product Promotion
Indiana University (19XX-19XX)
    a. Student, Graduate School of Business (carried 6 hours per semester)
    b. Assistant Director, Executive Education Program, Continuing Education
Chicago Trust and Savings Bank (19XX-19XX)
    Systems Analyst and computer programmer in Operations Dept.

EDUCATION

INDIANA UNIVERSITY SCHOOL OF BUSINESS
    a. MBA, Corporate Finance, 19XX   Minor: Systems
    b. BS, Accounting, 19XX   Minor: Marketing

Figure 4-9.

SAMPLE CAREER STATEMENTS

<u>Sales Representative</u>. Wish to begin my career in an assignment that offers contact with the public, structured on-the-job training, exposure to management, and a quality product or service. After training and some experience, I hope to move into management assignments involving training, personnel problems, advertising strategy, analyzing research studies, and supervising others.

<u>Industrial Sales Representative</u>. Desire a position that utilizes my technical background in physics, chemistry, and mathematics. Although not limited, industries most applicable include electronics, chemical, drugs, and oil. Special talents in aiding the technical interface between firm and customer. Aspire to become an operating marketing manager with responsibility for budgets, marketing plans, and decision-making responsibilities.

<u>Brand Assistant</u>. Want responsibility of coordinating advertising, pricing, packaging, forecasts, distribution channels, profits, etc. of a consumer goods product line. My pre-MBA sales experience should aid in coordinating programs with the sales force. Strong analytical skills and good writing skills coupled with experience hopefully will permit advancement to product manager.

<u>Sales Engineer</u>. Interested in industries such as electronics, electrical machinery, office products which can use my engineering training. Desire to serve as a technical service liaison with customer contact. Intermediate goal is to move into higher levels of responsibility from both a technical and managerial viewpoint.

<u>Retailing</u>. Interested in joining a department, chain, discount, or specialty store in a structured management training program. Prefer exposure to a wide variety of product or service lines. Desire experience in sales, supervision, buying, and other facets of retailing. Eventually hope to advance into either store management or the merchandising function.

<u>Public Relations Assistant</u>. Interested in copy writing, editing, writing speeches and news releases, photography, graphics, etc. Desire experience on organization's internal and external publications. My good writing and speaking skills with my communications background should assist in advancement to a management position within the public relations department.

<u>Personnel Assistant</u>. Expect to begin job in the personnel department of a unionized manufacturing concern where I can gain experience in the functions of labor contract administration, employment, compensation, benefit programs, training programs, and compliance regulations. Since long-term goal is to become a personnel manager, I need contact with each of the basic areas.

Figure 4-10.

SAMPLE CAREER STATEMENTS

<u>Accountant</u>. Considering opportunities in both public and industrial firms. Enjoy the client contact in public and the management potential in industry. Desire variety of experiences in auditing, cost, tax and finance. Based upon experience, long-term goal is to move into a chief financial office position or partner with a public firm.

<u>Industrial Accountant</u>. Plan to start with a manufacturing or service concern. Prefer on-the-job training in a variety of rotated assignments. Desire some experience in internal auditing, cost accounting, credit analysis, investment analysis, tax preparations, and the treasury functions. Eventual goal: chief financial officer.

<u>Public Accountant</u>. Desire to join a small to medium size firm where I can get training in auditing, taxes, and management service. Prefer a professional training oriented firm that keeps staff current through regular seminars and publications. Aspire to partnership within a reasonable period of time.

<u>Computer Specialist</u>. Plan to accept an initial job as a programmer or systems analyst which can make best use of my quantitative background. Interested in EDP manufacturers and software service firms. Special interest in marketing and finance applications. Prefer the role of systems consultant to several departments or customers.

<u>Financial Analyst</u>. Desire to join an organization that assigns complex financial projects to new employees immediately. Interested in analyzing projects involving capital cost, cash flow, capital investments, tax verifications, financing methods, pension fund security analysis, pricing, cost comparisons, profit and loss and balance sheet analysis, international consolidations, interest rates, monetary policy, etc. Eventually wish to move into the controllership function.

<u>Banking</u>. Goal is to become a senior bank operating officer. Initially desire to gain experience in branch management, operations, trust, and installment lending. Strongest thrust is in the commercial lending function where I can conduct complex credit analysis and meet commercial customers. At some point in my career path, an experience in international banking would be important.

<u>Production Assistant</u>. Goal is to start in any one of several areas in manufacturing including scheduling, industrial engineering, first line supervision, inventory control, physical distribution, purchasing, quality control, etc. Prefer an employer who permits one to rotate through various functions because eventually wish to move into operations management.

Figure 4-11.

gaining, strategy, labor laws, manpower planning and training, compensation, etc., may be listed.

Many graduates take courses or hold professional licenses obtained outside of the higher educational institutions. Students having passed a C.P.A. exam, a real estate license test, an insurance license exam, or if planning to take such a test, should document this information on the resume after listing the universities. Attendance in professional courses on computer programming, banking seminars, technical schools, and military training courses related to the professional objective should also be included. It is unwise to include every incidental course because eventually this may begin diluting the image of the degree.

Any publications or papers presented at professional meetings should be listed if they have a relation to the position for which applying. For a rather extensive list, it might be wise for the applicant to include only the most important and attach a list of publications desirable to use at the time of the interview. For some academic or consulting assignments, it may be desirable to attach a separate page to the resume.

College Activities. These activities are most likely to be important only for individuals with less than five years' work experience after graduation. For the recent college graduate this can be extremely important. These activities reveal certain values, concerns, and abilities to lead and command respect in a peer group. Each activity should be documented and discussed in concise detail. For example, if an applicant has been a varsity sport team member, the sport, participant semester(s), a statement of the position, time commitment, and responsibilities of the involvement should be identified. If work has limited participation in campus activities, omit this section completely.

Experience. The most widely accepted method of listing experience is in reverse chronological sequence (most recent first). The organization's name, position held, dates of employment, whether full or part-time, and the functions performed should always be shown. The highest level of work, not beginning assignments, should be described. If the name of the firm or its division is not widely known, a brief description of the firm as well as the applicant's duties, supervision responsibilities, financial responsibilities, and major accomplishments or projects completed can be indicated. It is becoming an accepted practice to include military service under work experience.

Many recent college graduates do not have much (if any) work experience that relates to the career objective. They need not be embarrassed because of lack of experience. One million graduates with little experience get jobs each year. In the work experience section of the resume, the employer is most likely looking to support the notion, "The applicant is a hard worker" rather than "The applicant has related experience." They want to know what was done with time not spent studying. Did the applicant make a contribution toward educational expenses? People who have worked full time one summer in a factory know that they have learned much about people and matured considerably. The employer recognizes this. People who have worked part-time while in school have picked up an education unavailable in books. The employer knows this. It is not necessary to spell out every little job on a resume, but it is necessary to present a representative sample of important work experience. Spelling out some of the menial tasks that have been performed to meet a major objective toward which the applicant has worked—the degree, says much about one's qualities and values.

Miscellaneous. It may be advantageous to iden-

COLLEGE/CIVIC ACTIVITIES

Group Participation

Academic Assistant
Academic Clubs/Groups
Bands and Orchestras
Campus Newspapers
Campus Political Party
Dorm Organization
Ethnic Organizations
Fraternities
Interfraternal Groups
Professional Associations
Scholastic Fraternities
Singing Groups
Sororities
Technical Societies
Union Boards
Women's Organizations
Yearbook Programs

Noncampus Groups

Big Brothers/Sisters
Commerce
Flying Clubs
Foundations
4-H Clubs
Hospital Aide
Junior Achievement
Music Societies
Nonprofit Organizations
Religious Organizations
Scouting
Service Clubs
Social Work
Teacher's Aide
United Funds
Youth Groups
Youth Sports

Sports: Varsity/Intramural

Archery
Baseball
Basketball
Football
Golf
Gymnastics
Handball
Lacrosse
Polo
Racquetball
Rowing
Rugby
Soccer
Swimming
Tennis
Track
Volleyball

Leadership Roles

Board Member
President
Representative
Secretary
Staff Assistant
Treasurer
Vice-president

Committees

Alumni
Curriculum
Commencement
Foundation
Homecoming
Major Events
Steering

Political

Campus Politics
League of Voters
Lobbying
Precinct Worker
Young Democrats
Young Republicans
Voter Registration

Figure 4-12.

tify specific background, professional associations, hobbies, outside interests, special skills, spouse's background, etc. This could include various parts of the country lived in, the extent to which one is well traveled, conservation clubs, volunteer services, junior achievement, Jaycee's, church affiliation (if a leader), father's occupation, and any other points that indicate positive reasons why a firm might be interested in the applicant for career assignment.

References. Many resume experts now recommend one simply to state, "References furnished on request." Good references are not all that common, however, so when an applicant has gone to the trouble of obtaining permission from three or four people known well, their potential influence with employers should be utilized. Many teachers (at least two faculty members should have been cultivated), neighbors, and friends of the family are flattered to be asked to write personal letters of reference. Many are happy to provide a "to whom it may concern" reference letter. These letters can be used at the time of the interview as a part of the presentation.

People should be selected who are familiar with the applicant's academic and work capabilities. Those people with as high a professional standing as possible should be selected. Professors, bankers, teachers, community leaders, former employers, business owners, sales or financial managers, lawyers, and individuals employed in the career field sought are excellent references. The reason that references are not used as often as they once were is because employers rarely see negative remarks. But a positive reference cannot hurt and may be the item that obtains the interview.

Another good reason for including references is that the person receiving the resume may personally

know one of your references. In such cases a telephone call by the employer to the reference almost insures getting a personal interview. By careful planning of the resume distribution this approach can work more than by chance alone.

If the resume length is approaching two pages and references are the item that forces the two pages, it might be better to omit references. Most employers do not contact references before the initial interview. As necessary, references can be provided at the time of the interview.

References listed on a resume simply say that others of important stature know you well and are willing to say so. Many individuals go through college and life without recognizing the importance of personal contacts. Whether contacted or not, references listed on a resume offer important information to potential employers.

Improving the Resume

There are many ways by which the resume can be improved and just as many ideas on what to do on one. Already discussed is the idea of slanting the resume toward the exact position which is known to be open. Applicants should use some empathy to appreciate the point of view of the employer. This involves an interpretation of the characteristics felt to be important in the job and then stressing those points in the resume. This technique might best be appropriate when there is one special job desired above all others.

Applicants should avoid unnecessary data. They must emphasize essential information only, but make certain the resume is complete and is well spaced on the one page. Unnecessary words such as "I" and "he" should be eliminated, and whenever possible, a sentence should start with a verb or action word.

Figure 4-13 gives some of these key words. The list also identifies important words to use to develop a positive image.

Eye appeal should be emphasized. Even using a typewriter, it is necessary to use some artistic talent in designing a resume that appeals as well as tells. The resume should be uncluttered, neatly blocked and organized so that key points are quickly zeroed in on by the reader. It should include numbers (people and dollars) to indicate responsibility levels in college activities and work.

The resume should not become too unconventional in the physical makeup. Most employers still prefer an 8 1/2 by 11 inch page on high quality paper rather than an odd size that must be folded to be filed. No mileage is gained in irritating the prospective employer. Cover sheets, fancy folds, gimmicks, and odd-toned paper should be omitted because these fool few professional personnel people.

The resume should be a credit to the individual's creativity and ability in self-expression. It is an advertisement designed to sell the applicant's ability and potential rather than just experience and schooling.

Over 95% of all employment hires are introduced by a resume so care *must* be used in constructing it. It should focus on what *can and will* be done for the employer based upon the evidence of past accomplishments presented. One should rely on positive results from past activities even if it is necessary to go into major classroom projects in which a major lead was played.

To close, review these don'ts. Don't . . . state salary requirements, give reasons for changing past employers, limit the geographic considerations unless absolutely necessary (do so only if essential), send the resume with typographical errors, get personal, expound on philosophy or values, let someone else pre-

pare the resume. With this information, the applicant can proceed to develop communication tool number one!

COVER LETTERS

The chances of landing a job solely on the basis of a resume and cover letter (also called a letter of application) are practically nil. The purpose of a cover letter is to introduce the individual (and accompanying qualifications through the attached resume) to a prospective employer and to obtain an interview appointment or application blank.

A good letter creates the desire in the employer to read the resume and the urge to talk with the applicant. It also clues the employer on written communication skills. Cover letters are read, compared, and used to screen applicants for possibilities for further consideration. More should not be expected from them. A piece of paper should not do any more than provide a chance to present one's case in person.

Personnel officers receive many more letters from potential applicants than they could ever interview. They receive hundreds of unsolicited letters each day from college graduates and a typical want ad may produce as many as 2,000 replies. The letter and attached resume are used to screen candidates. Only a carefully worded, concisely detailed letter stands a chance of getting through the screening maze. At the same time, a high percentage of college hires result from this procedure.

Use of the Cover Letter

The cover letter should not reiterate everything in the resume. It must complement and expand upon the resume and support a position on why the applicant should be considered further. The cover letter will serve as an introduction before walking into an office to apply for a specific job.

Cover letters are usually sent as a result of a referral by a third party (faculty member, friend, agency, etc.), an advertisement of the opening, or simply a blind, unsolicited inquiry. There is no necessity for a cover letter before on-campus interviews, telephone referrals to employers where there is already an appointment, or where it is preferred to walk into the personnel office.

When conducting a "direct mail" letter campaign, a "rifle" or "shotgun" approach to the campaign can be taken. In a "rifle" campaign, a list of selected employers who normally have openings in one area of interest is used to initiate contact. From placement offices, want ads, faculty, and friends, letters can be aimed at employers with specifically known openings. The problem here is that an extensive list of potential contacts may not be available.

In a "shotgun" campaign, letters are mailed to many employers in an attempt to develop openings or stumble upon solid leads. Contacts are taken from the *College Placement Annual,* telephone directories, and other trade or professional rosters. With today's mailing rates, this is an expensive approach, but it may be the only recourse in some job markets and career fields. The typical response to a normal 100 letter mailing is about four or five replies saying that the employer will be happy to set up an interview when the applicant is in the employer's geographical area. Most firms will not even send a negative response because of the hundreds of letters recieved. One innovative, but expensive, idea is to include a self-addressed stamped reply card where the employer has only to check a given response box (no opening, have opening—will interview, or will interview for later consideration if opening develops).

Preparation of Cover Letters

All letters of application should be personalized to be most effective. An obviously reproduced form

KEY WORDS FOR RESUME AND COVER LETTER PREPARATION
Action Words

actively	delegate	generate	motivated	proficient	significantly
accelerated	develop	increased	organize	recommend	simplicity
adapted	demonstrate	influence	originate	reduced	set up
administer	direct	implemented	participated	reinforced	solve
analyze	effect	interpret	perform	reorganized	strategy
approve	eliminated	improve	plan	revamped	structure
coordinate	established	launched	pinpointed	responsible	streamline
conceived	evaluate	lead	program	responsibilities	successfully
conduct	expanded	lecture	proposed	revise	supervise
completed	expedite	maintain	proved	review	support
control	founded	manage	provide	schedule	teach
created					

Self-Descriptive Words

active	consistent	efficient	logical	positive	sense-of-humor
adaptable	constructive	energetic	loyal	practical	sincere
aggressive	creative	enterprising	mature	productive	sophisticated
alert	dependable	enthusiastic	methodical	realistic	systematic
ambitious	determined	extroverted	objective	reliable	tactful
analytical	diplomatic	fair	optimistic	resourceful	talented
attentive	disciplined	forceful	perceptive	respective	will travel
broad-minded	discrete	imaginative	personable	self-reliant	will relocate
conscientious	economical	independent	pleasant		

Figure 4-13.

letter should never be sent. The placement office or a number of directories in libraries can supply names of persons to contact, preferably employment managers or supervisors in departments of interest. As a last resort, a functional title such as Personnel Director, Sales Manager, or President, if it is a very small firm, can be used.

A number of examples in the book give typical cover letter formats. Unlike the resume, a preprinted letter is unacceptable.

The cover letter should never exceed one page. Emphasis is placed upon facts and brevity. In the applicant's own style, it is necessary to say, "I am interested in you; here is why you should be interested in me; can I have an interview appointment?" Sounds simple—it isn't!

Introduction. The first paragraph must attract attention. The reason for writing should be stated by naming the position for which applying, and how the opening was heard of or how the employer's name was obtained. One technique is to straightforwardly ask in the opening sentence a question, "Are you interested in employing a hard working, energetic and aggressive recent college graduate in a sales position? I have the personality and ambition to advance into

marketing management in a few years." Whatever the opening, the letter must spark enough interest to cause the employer to want to press forward.

Body. In the second paragraph the reason is stated for writing to this particular employer and for wanting to work for the organization. Concrete reasons should be emphasized and flowery phrases describing growth, challenge, advancement, etc., avoided. In this paragraph, the applicant's specific challenges and aspirations should be mentioned. *Why* success can be achieved should be supported. How education and past achievements will support the capacity for which consideration is desired must be indicated.

Some of the key words in Figure 4-13 to describe accomplishments may be utilized. The resume data should not be repeated any more than is absolutely necessary. Only a few seconds are available to capture the employer's imagination, so wasted words must be avoided. The meat of the resume should be emphasized and personal qualities documented.

The third paragraph should be short and refer to the resume. It should emphasize career interest and personal qualities. This message must get through! For a third party referral, or mutual acquaintance, the party's name and how highly the company was recommended should be stated. Wanting to work for *that* employer must be emphasized!

Close. The closing paragraph is just as important as the opening. The response desired should be stated. Phrases like "if you have further interest, please write," should be avoided. Since the purpose is to get an interview, it should be requested in this paragraph.

One very positive response is to state that a call to the firm will be made on a specific date to arrange a specific time. Few people will turn down the call. Often it is wise to tell the employer that plans to be in the area during a certain week have been made and that a call for an appointment will be made at the end of the preceding or the beginning of the next week. Arrival of the letter should be timed so that it arrives one or two days before the call and five to ten work days before the visit to the firm's community, if it is different than the applicant's.

If requesting information concerning the existence of an opening, the applicant should end the cover letter with a specific question.

Few employers are likely to encourage applicants, unseen, to come in for appointments if it is necessary to travel more than 50 miles. Qualified applicants may be waiting in the lobby so employers would hesitate to hedge on the inquiry; therefore, the initiative must be taken by the applicant after sending the letter. However, it is not desirable to force a "no" decision without getting a chance for a personal presentation of one's qualifications.

Summary. The cover letter is likely to get a favorable response if it contains a tone of modest confidence. The closing paragraph might, therefore, assume that the employer is interested and that the next logical step is an appointment. Asking for a specific day for an appointment is another approach. Still

another idea is to ask for information on specific jobs, a job description, an employment brochure, or an application blank. Keeping the reader in mind when writing the letter and keeping the letter concise by focusing on a specific position, gives an idea of what might be done if the applicant were the employer. Is the letter effective enough to elicit a written positive response if an opening exists? With the cover letter and resume finished, most of the written communication is complete. Preparing an interview presentation is the next step.

LOCATING JOB OPPORTUNITIES

The best cover letter and resume are effective only if they reach the proper person. Researching and locating employers whose needs best fit a graduate's qualifications are essential to a sound career plan. Job leads are most often found through direct contacts with employers and through contacts through a third party. The college placement office is the primary source to begin the task of locating potential employers. Other third party sources include friends, faculty, newspaper advertisements, and public and private employment agencies.

College Placement Offices

The College Placement Office is an organization located on campus with the express purpose of getting potential employers together with potential candidates. Depending upon the university, services provided vary widely, but most of them offer some form of on-campus interviewing with employers.

Many placement offices provide rather extensive aids to assist graduates in their career planning projects. Most have facilities available where future applicants can read employment brochures from employers, annual reports, current job listings, and descriptions of hundreds of jobs as well as the standard sources of names for various employing organizations. There are seldom any charges for placement assistance (except for resume and credential reproduction) to either the registrant or the employer.

Most of the major employers in the United States work through and cooperate fully with college placement offices. Both are members of a nonprofit professional organization called the College Placement Council. The Council publishes a code of ethics to which both parties subscribe. Many of the forms, such as the College Interview Form, are jointly developed by the parties and are standardized throughout the nation.

Campus Interviews. For most graduates, on-campus interviewing is the easiest and most effective means for landing the first assignment after college.

PREFERRED PROCEDURE FOR CONTACTING EMPLOYERS	
Write Letter/Enclose Resume	95%
Write Complete Letter	60
Work Through a Third Party	32
Telephone for Appointment	26
Walk in Office Unannounced	15
Contact Nonpersonnel Executive	2

Based on survey of 185 employers in 1972 Endicott Report.

Figure 4-14.

Apartment 22
Stone Hill Estates
Arcola, Ohio 32064
February 17, 19XX

Mr. G. B. Executive
Personnel Department
Professional Pharmaceuticals
Middletown, Michigan 47720

Dear Mr. Executive

   Do you have an opening for a sales representative? With a B.S. degree
in marketing and ten hours of chemistry courses at Ohio State University,
I think that my academic qualifications and personality are well suited for
a career in pharmaceutical marketing.

   Two summers and many part-time jobs in sales-related positions have
convinced me that sales is the best entry-level position for me to begin my
career as a future marketing executive. I value the freedom and independence that you offer an individual after your training program which I
read about in the College Placement Office. Each of my previous employers
will tell you that I work hard and thrive under pressure and challenge.
Although I have not been active in campus life as a leader because I had
to work to get through school, every work supervisor has expressed pleasure
at my enthusiasm to serve customers.

   In my last experience at Super Drugs, I worked for a pharmacist and
talked with several salesmen who called on us. They all commented on the
individual rewards of working in the booming health-related industry. The
attached resume only brushes the surface of my qualifications so I hope I
have the opportunity to elaborate in person on my credentials.

   I am willing to work hard, study, learn, and take responsibility. May
I have the privilege of an interview? Since we are several hundred miles
apart, would it be possible for me to schedule an initial interview with
any of your salesmen in this region? I plan to call you within the week to
see if something might possibly be arranged. I need a chance to start as a
sales representative because I know I can advance on my own merits with
Professional Pharmaceuticals. Please call me if you need more information.

                          Very truly yours

                          Morris Catt

                          Morris Catt

Enclosure

Figure 4-15.

1400 N. Maple Lane
Bloomington, IN 47401
September 13, 19XX

Ms. U. R. Fashion
Manager, Organizational Development
High Fashion Stores, Inc.
Chicago, IL 60601

Dear Ms. Fashion:

I received your name from the placement office at Indiana University where I am earning a bachelor degree in English. Ms. Smith encouraged me to write you about being considered for your executive development program which starts in June.

Although I am not a business graduate, I have many of the other qualifications which you outlined in some information I found in the placement office. I have been involved in a leadership capacity in several activities on campus and have worked as a part-time sales clerk in a local coed specialty shop for the past year. I am familiar with the basic retail sales functions of display, marking, inventories, cash control, advertising, etc. from the sales clerk point of view.

I really enjoy the public contact and servicing the customer but I want to get more experience in the buying function, supervision, and general administration. As vice president of my sorority, I learned much about management skills. This encouraged me to take two courses in business (accounting and retail marketing) which should help my understanding of your business operations. I hope to graduate in the top twenty percent of my class. My resume is enclosed.

I hope that we can get together. My personal plans call for a trip to Chicago later next month. Would it be possible for us to meet on February 20? I will call you or your secretary next Tuesday to set up a specific appointment time. Please feel free to call me at 812-336-5561 if that date is inconvenient. I appreciate your consideration.

Sincerely yours,

Susan Outgoing

Susan Outgoing

Enclosures

Figure 4-16.

Rock Berry Hall
Evansville, Illinois
May 15, 19XX

Mr. J. B. Price
Labor Relations Manager
Golden Enterprises, Inc.
Chicago, Illinois 60121

Dear Mr. Price:

Dr. C. Randall Powell, Professor of Business Administration at Indiana
University, recently suggested that I write you concerning your opening
and my interest in a labor relations assistant position. With a B.S.
degree in personnel management and courses in labor economics, collective
bargaining, and labor law, I am confident that I could make a positive
contribution to the opportunity.

The last two summers, I worked as a general laborer on a production line,
once in a unionized shop and once in an unorganized plant. My ability to
appreciate several points of view on labor problems should prove to be a
major asset in my future career performance. Before I left my last summer
job, my supervisor had recommended that I be hired as a first-line foreman
after graduation. Although I am enthusiastic about the foreman's position,
I think my energies and resourcefulness might be better suited to tactfully
handling union-management problems as a third party in the grievance steps.
This assignment has been a four-year goal for me in college.

My attached resume better highlights my education and experience. My leadership roles in campus politics should strengthen and support my abilities to
serve as a labor relations assistant.

I am anxious to talk with you because I feel I can show you why I am a strong
candidate for the position. I have friends in Chicago that I could stay with
on weekends so any Friday or Monday would be ideal for an appointment. In
three days I will call you to see if your schedule might be open. I look
forward to us getting together soon. If you need additional information,
please call or write me or Dr. Powell.

Very truly yours,

James J. Aggressive

James J. Aggressive

Enclosure

Figure 4-17.

R. R. 13, Box 64
Minniville, Ohio 34260
December 10, 19XX

Mr. J. Paul Big
Manager of College Relations
Gusher Petroleum
Houston, Texas

Dear Mr. Big:

Your advertisement in the <u>College Placement Annual</u> prompted me to write you inquiring about consideration for a position in chemical engineering. I will receive a bachelor of science degree in biology from Ohio State University in June.

Before you pitch this letter because I am not an engineer, please take a look at my credentials on the enclosed resume. I rank near the top of my class, am senior class president, captain of the reserve rugby team, experienced in laboratory techniques, and organized and supervised a student government project of leasing mini-refrigerators to dorm residents.

I have read the job description of a chemical engineer from employment brochures in the placement office for companies in the drug, chemical, petroleum, and agri-business industries. I have also reviewed some engineering textbooks of my chemical engineering friends. I have the background and interest to handle all work assignments even though I don't have the exact degree you are seeking.

My background consists of 18 hours of chemistry, 6 hours in physics, 12 hours in math, and 30 hours in the biological sciences. My advisor, Dr. I. M. Smart, is encouraging me to go to graduate school, but I am more interested in utilizing my background in a practical setting instead of a research orientation. I also have interests in quality control and production supervision of technical products.

I prefer to locate in your area and am trying to determine if a 1,000 mile trip in late January is worth the cost. I do have relatives with whom I can stay. Enclosed is a copy of this letter with a stamped and addressed envelope. If you can offer the slightest encouragement to me, I am willing to pay for a trip to the area. Please check the appropriate boxes and return. I shall look forward to your reply and hopefully a personal interview. Thank you for your interest and consideration.

Very truly yours,

C. U. Around

C. U. Around

☐ Call for an appointment   ☐ Recontact in __ weeks
☐ Stop in when get here   ☐ No present background match
☐ Call when arrive in town   ☐ Return application blank

Encl.

Figure 4-18.

Pleasant View Hall
Floyd Knobs, Indiana
February 24, 19XX

Mr. J. B. Money, President
First National Bank
First and Walnut
Hoosierland, Indiana 45201

Dear Mr. Money:

In reply to your classified ad in the Hoosier Banker, I would like to apply
for the Branch Manager trainee position. I graduated from DePauw University
with an economics major in December.

Because of some part-time work experience in related areas and academic
courses in the field, I am very familiar with the various assignments in
banking which is my basic career interest. I read the book, Money Changers,
a few years ago which was recommended by a professor here and was very
unhappy with the journalistics liberties taken by Mr. Haley, but I learned
a lot which stimulated my interest. The recent article in Fortune Magazine
on women officers in banking convinced me that I made the right decision.

During my first three years at DePauw, I worked as a part-time teller at the
University Credit Union. During summers I worked as a clerk/secretary basically filling in as vacation relief in several jobs. Beginning my senior
year I worked part-time in the Bursar's Office doing odd jobs dealing with
cash balances, fee collections, auditing statements, calling on bad debts,
report writing, etc. I have taken courses in money and banking, financial
institutions and two courses in accounting and finance which I took at
night school during summers at home.

Because of my interest in locating in a smaller community like yours, I am
especially interested in your job. Although it is three months before graduation, I want to make a decision fairly soon. Would you please send me an
application and more information about the job and community. I am available for an interview any Monday or Friday, which are my lightest class days.
I will call you for an appointment as soon as I receive the application.

Sincerely yours,

Jane Career

Jane Career

Figure 4-19.

421 E. Fourteenth St.
Apt. H-4
Bloomington, IN 47401
April 2, 19XX

Mr. U. I. Alumnus
Partner
CPA & Associates
Woodward and High Sts.
Detroit, MI 38251

Dear Mr. Alumnus

My accounting professor, Dr. Curt Brown, was recently counselling me on my interest in joining a small public accounting firm in the Detroit area. I expect to receive a bachelor degree in accounting from Notre Dame in June. Professor Brown said that you might be able to offer some guidance since you had the same problem a few years ago.

I have not been an academic superstar but I have never earned anything less than a "B" grade in accounting, either. I have worked 20 hours each week as a night auditor for the University Union for the past two years which has limited my extra-curricular activities, but working got me through college. During my first two years here, I got quite involved in organizing an intra-mural softball league for women, but wound up umpiring because I needed the money.

Because my fiance has found an excellent job opportunity with an automotive firm, we have decided to locate in the Detroit area. I am interested in joining a small to medium size public accounting firm. Since few firms that size actively recruit, I need some help in identifying some of the better prospects in the area. My enclosed resume explains why I think I am best suited for this type of firm.

Enclosed is a stamped, self-addressed envelope. Could you take a minute of your time to jot down some appropriate contacts for me? Based on Dr. Brown's comments, I would especially be interested in learning more about your firm. If you think that there is a chance for employment in your firm, would you please give me a collect call? I can get to Detroit on a day's notice. I thank you in advance for any help you can give.

Sincerely

I. O. U. Favors

I. O. U. Favors

Enclosure

Figure 4-20.

301 N. Indiana Avenue
Bloomington, IN 47401
October 4, 19XX

Mr. A. G. President
President
President Advertising Agency
1000 N. Michigan
Chicago, IL 60604

Dear Mr. President:

Advertising's my bag and I'm ready for your game. Aim at me if you want a
self-starter and go-getter. For a job as a copy writer/account executive,
I offer the following credentials.

- Degree in communications
- Top grades
- Marketing orientation
- Leadership potential

- Gregarious personality
- Pleasing appearance
- Aggressiveness
- Determination

They tell me that no jobs exist in advertising unless you know somebody
who knows somebody important. Unfortunately, the important people who know
me don't know you. But I'm important and want to work for you.

Getting a job in advertising is exciting, challenging, and real hard work.
It is really testing my communication skills.

Notice the advertising brochure on Roger (some call it a resume). This
tacky approach is unique, original, funny, yet truthful and I hope it gets
my foot into your door. The ad I wrote for <u>Advertising Age</u> cost too much
to print and my old resume wasn't me and hit too many circular files. I'm
bettin' on this approach.

I want to work for you and need an interview. You can contact me by returning
the handy tear-away order form on the resume brochure (the enclosed coupon
will get you a discount). I would like to hear from you soon. To avoid
C.O.D. charges, you can expedite matters by calling 812-337-6660 collect today.

Very truly yours,

R. U. Funn

R. U. Funn

Enclosure

Figure 4-21.

Employers often prefer to fill their needs through on-campus interviewing because they can see large numbers of applicants at a time; it is inexpensive as compared to other means; and they see the top talent in the nation first.

Some employers will have hundreds of job openings located throughout the country. College recruiting is usually national in scope and large employers can refer graduates to several different locations after initial on-campus interviews. Other methods of employment are localized and applicants must be available in the geographical area of the opening. Often an employer will pay for transportation to a second interview that is 200 or 300 miles away.

Teams of college recruiters usually visit campuses during the fall months of October, November, and December for students graduating at midyear. During the spring, they are on campuses during January, February, and March to hire the June and summer graduates. Although the policies at schools differ some, most June graduates will register for placement assistance near the beginning of the last year in school. Many take interviews both in the fall and spring periods.

Students who wait until one or two months before graduation to contact employers have a very tough time finding employment. An early start is the secret. Employers often try to fill all of their openings through college recruiting by April; therefore, there are few professional jobs left for late applicants. Those individuals about to graduate must plan early for the better opportunities!

Referrals. Not all placement offices operate extensive on-campus college recruiting programs. The number of graduates may not be large enough to attract large numbers of employers, and the mix of academic majors may not be in high demand fields. The role of the placement director in small colleges and liberal arts schools is somewhat different than that in large universities and in business and engineering curriculums.

Directors at these institutions maintain close touch with alumni, local employers, and personal relationships with a selected group of national employers. Referrals to job possibilities is done on a personal basis. In such schools, graduates must get to know the placement staff on a personal basis. Only if the staff knows an individual will they place their credibility on the line with employers.

The one-on-one personal referral basis can be just as effective, often more effective, as the mass interviewing. The referral approach accomplishes the same goal: It gets candidates interviews, not jobs. Only effective interviews translate into jobs, and that topic is discussed in the next chapter.

Service. The placement office should not be viewed simply as an agency that lines up interviews. The key behind finding success in a career assignment lies in prior preparation. Only a graduate can do this preparation. The placement office can assist the graduate in many ways by offering job search advice, job leads, and personal counseling. The job hunting wheel has been invented, but too many graduates insist on making the same logical mistakes as their predecessors. The placement staff offers a unique service that teaches effective career planning principles and career search techniques.

Other Sources of Contacts

Not all employers recruit on campus. Many prefer to send placement officers a list of their openings every month or so. Others send a special letter, telegram, or telephone when an opening requiring an inexperienced graduate materializes. All placement offices publish and/or post all of these openings with the information necessary to contact the employer directly. The placement bulletin boards should be watched constantly.

The placement office distributes the most informative book on employers available, *The College Placement Annual.* This book is available free only from the placement office. Some libraries get copies. It gives the current name and address of the person to contact in over 2000 employing organizations. Many employers advertise in it. The "big yellow book" identifies types of positions, employers, and is cross classified by college major and geographical location. The *Annual* is not a list of openings, but it does represent the employer's best guess of what will be available. The placement officer provides this source!

Placement offices keep a wide variety of literature available for reference. Most major government and corporate employers keep placement offices well supplied with recruitment brochures. Even for new graduates undecided about a career, these can be helpful because they often discuss the duties, responsibilities, future potential, and qualifications for many different types of openings. The pictures and descriptive materials may help focus on a given field.

Most offices also have on reference a copy of the Department of Labor's, three-inch thick, *Occupational Outlook Handbook,* and the special edition of it which is directed to college graduates. The *Handbook* contains several hundred job titles with descriptions for all jobs included in it of the work involved, the places of employment, qualifications, earnings, employment outlook, and sources of additional information. It is a useful planning tool.

A working relationship with the placement officer(s) should be cultivated. They personally know hundreds of employers and a recommendation can often secure an offer. Their potential aid and influence should not be underestimated. But relying solely on the placement office is wrong because there are such wide varieties of sources for employment leads. All of them should be used for an effective campaign.

Personal Contacts. Contacting faculty, friends, acquaintances, and relatives is a process not to be overlooked. In a national survey of recent graduates who were employed, a high percentage obtained their employment this way.

A contact list should be methodically developed. It should be narrowed to those who may have some reason to happen across job openings in the field of interest selected. These people should be provided with a letter explaining the position being sought and asking for their help. A copy of the resume should be included. This process should commence about five months before graduation, and these contacts should be kept current on job status. By sending them similar notes each month until obtaining employment, their interest will be maintained.

Publications. Employers often have a difficult time finding qualified talent even in weak job market periods. Even during recessions, each day there are hundreds of opportunities advertised in numerous newspapers, trade journals, and professional publications. Plans to scan the classified ads in the major metropolitan areas within the geographical area of interest should be developed. Libraries often carry out-of-town papers and the professional and trade journals, such as the *Wall Street Journal, Automotive News, InfoSystems,* etc. Even when not matching the desired qualifications exactly as specified, an individual should not hesitate to write or call (follow their instructions). An applicant is unlikely to find a perfect match, and a compromise often proves to be acceptable to the employer.

Third Party Assistance

Employment Service. The state employment offices in many cities are taking an increasing interest in

---

CONTACT GENERATORS

College Placement Office
Private Employment Agency
Public Employment Service
Faculty
Friends
Directories
Advertisements

Figure 4-22.

CONTACTS

1. Get Resumes Read
2. Arrange Interviews
3. Make Introductions
4. Give Recommendations
5. Cannot Hire People

Figure 4-23.

```
┌─────────────────────────────────────────┐
│                                         │
│      CONTACT REFERENCE PUBLICATIONS     │
│                                         │
│      College Placement Annual           │
│      Dictionary of Occupational Titles  │
│      Occupational Outlook Handbook      │
│      Federal Careers                    │
│      World Wide Chamber of Commerce Directory │
│      Thomas Register of American Manufacturers │
│      Encyclopedia of Associations       │
│      Moody's Industrial Manual          │
│      Guide to American Directories      │
│      Trade Association Magazines        │
│      Professional Association Directories │
│                                         │
└─────────────────────────────────────────┘
```

Figure 4-24.

professional and managerial employment. Many employers are forced to list openings with them because of veteran preferences and minority employment laws if the employers have certain government contracts. The services are free to both the employer and the applicant and offices are located in most major towns.

Agencies. Private employment agencies or search firms should not be overlooked. Even if it costs the normal 10% of the first year's salary it may be worth it. In fields where the labor market is very tight, the employer may even pay the fee.

In simplest terms, an employment counselor is a person who maintains two files: one of job openings and one of applicants. In a perfect world these two lists would match, but in fact this seldom happens. Consequently, the employment counselor many times becomes a salesperson working for two parties at the same time. The counselor may have to convince the applicant to take a job which requires fewer skills than the applicant possesses (downgrade), and/or to convince the employer to accept a compromise applicant. Counselors are often caught in the role of a salesperson because they work on commission and make their living only when creating job/applicant matches.

Agencies build up their files by placing newspaper ads offering nice sounding jobs to stimulate the applicant's interest. These firms build up job files by calling, or direct mailing, employers on a regular basis asking for openings. Many such firms supplement their placement business by having applicants sign contracts for certain resume, testing, and counseling services. Even if employers pay the placement fees, applicants pay for the services. Registration fees are considered unethical. Before signing a contract, it is necessary for the applicant to ask about these items and what is expected if the job does not work out after a few weeks.

An applicant seeking a job in a given city should stop in and talk with *several* agencies. Registering with two or three firms can be productive. It is recommended that the applicant talk to the placement officer about different agencies. The experience of placement officers varies considerably. One agency in Indianapolis may be effective and professional but the same agency in Chicago may be questionable. Even within the same agency in a given city experience may vary depending upon the particular counselor working on a case. When, after the visit and interview, the counselor has displayed a fair appreciation and concern for the applicant's welfare and position, the decision to register with the firm can be made. Each visit is an individual decision.

To be sure, it is rough to be out of work; but it is tougher to be under a great new debt (about $1,000-2,000 normally). Applicants should be resourceful and do as much digging as possible. Resourcefulness can be enhanced by using the placement office, newspapers, direct mail, telephone, faculty, friends, and professional trade associations as much as possible. Many employers will think more of one's initiative if the individual lands the job without help. When frustrated, however, asking for professional help from an agency is recommended.

Career Conferences. Another alternative that should be considered is a new idea called "career conferences." These are placement programs most often sponsored by such organizations as the hometown Chamber of Commerce. The idea is that cities wish to attract the best of their youth who went away to college back to the community. The Chamber (or other groups) organizes local employers into a two or three day interviewing program, usually held between Christmas and New Year's, and invite returning college graduates to a program at a local hotel. Usually thirty minute interview arrangements are made the first day of the conference. This information can be obtained by writing the local Chamber of Commerce for details and checking with the college placement officer.

Search Firms. Do not confuse employment agencies and search firms. Search firms contract with employers to find a person for a given job assignment. The jobs are almost over $25,000 and require extensive experience. The employer often pays the search firm whether or not the job search is successful. Search firms do not "register" potential job candidates as agencies do. The responsibility is to the employer and they aggressively search out qualified

applicants whether or not the best qualified person is in the job market. Search firms receive hundreds of resumes each week, most of which are pitched. Search firms are not for recent college graduates.

Summary

Several approaches have been suggested for locating and contacting potential employers. The ropes and procedures are now evident but before leaping into the process, it is necessary to plan for the initial interview.

The self-assessment, career exploration, job campaign strategy, the cover letter, and the resume take a considerable amount of time to plan. A verbal presentation in an interview will take much time also. A final exam should not be taken without many hours of preparation. Why approach possibly the most important thirty minutes of one's life without a sound study plan? The time invested will pay off!

5

INTERVIEWING:
Preparation—Presentation—Technique

The development of the proper tools necessary to obtain the interview requires considerable time and effort. The resume concisely summarizes background so that essentials can be readily identified. The interview is not the place to restate the resume. Employers can read! The applicant should dive into the meat of the resume (the strongest points) and expand upon them. The resume is a written presentation of an applicant's credentials while the interview is an oral presentation of them.

A good recruiter is interested in what makes applicants think and react and, more importantly, why they behave as they do. The interviewer will want to probe into the major activities listed on the resume so they can appraise the type of qualities not revealed on a piece of paper. What motivates applicants? What are their values? What types of personality do they present? Are their verbal expression abilities consistent with their background? Are they leaders or followers? What excites them? What are their ambitions? How much thinking have they done about their career plans? What can they offer? What are they willing to do?

Development of the Presentation

The secret to successful interviewing is a sound presentation. All successful salespeople develop personal presentations. A good presentation requires preparation—much preparation. By following the career planning strategies as presented, a major step has been taken in the presentation: the self-assessment. A successful recruiter has been trained to probe until an appreciation of both strong and weak qualities of the applicant have been established.

Applicants who do their own self-assessment know conclusions interviewers will likely make. Knowing what the interviewer is likely to find makes it relatively easy to direct the interview toward one's strengths rather than one's weaknesses. Instead of offering explanations and apologies for weak points, the initiative should be taken and assets presented.

Many employers will not be expert interviewers. In this situation, a well-prepared presentation is most important because some recruiters emphasize reasons why *not* to hire. Applicants should plan to support reasons why they *should* be hired. The effective presentation points to why the applicant should be hired.

Why hire a particular applicant? If this question cannot be answered, the applicant is not the person for the job. Regardless of background, one can make a strong verbal presentation for a given assignment if advance preparation is done.

Preparation involves homework about oneself. It also involves homework about the employer. Annual reports, investment services, faculty, friends, employment brochures, and present employees can all help. If it is known what the firm is seeking, the presentation should be geared to zero in on all the strong points that are relevant. Figure 5-1 identifies some of the information one should have on the employer before going to the interview. Where it is impossible (after great searching) to obtain this type of information, the applicant should request some of it in the interview. Applicants having this information in advance of the interview can spend an hour or two developing a presentation that will interweave their background and interests into what the employer has to offer.

Being knowledgeable about the employer before the interview leaves the applicant free to explore other possibilities in the interview. If the employer is providing information that should already have been obtained, little is being done about why the applicant should be considered further. The employer is there to evaluate the applicant. An applicant can evaluate an employer after getting an invitation for an in-depth interview or after receiving an offer. Interest can be shown by asking relevant and pertinent questions, so it is necessary to develop a presentation that includes questions requiring specific answers about the employer.

Interview Factors Evaluated

Several faculty members at a major university recently conducted a survey of about 200 major corporate employers with the purpose of learning more

---

Information to Have on the Employer

Relative size of firm in the industry
Potential growth for the industry
Percent of annual sales growth the last five years
Array of product line or services
Potential new markets, products, or services
Various price points in product or service line
Who is the competition
Age of top management
Organization structure—by product line, functional, etc.
Geographical locations
Number of plants, stores, or sales outlets
Short-term profit picture
Structure or unstructured training
Average time in non-management assignment
Recent items in the news
Structure of assets
Relocation policies
Percent of annual growth in earnings per share
Present price of stock
People you know in the firm
Formal versus on-the-job training
Typical career path in your field
Location of home office
Name of recruiter

Figure 5-1.

---

about employer attitudes toward the on-campus interview. How important is the interview? Three-fourths rated the interview of primary importance and one-fourth attached equal weight to both the interview and resume. Clearly, a sound resume and an effective interview presentation are both needed. Sixty percent acknowledged that the recruiter's impressions, based on resume and interview, of the candidate are paramount in the employment decision; however, 25% put more weight on the skills, particularly in the hiring of engineers, accountants, etc. Almost 80% viewed the interview as a screening device, not a selling the organization role.

Once a skill match is made (candidate's abilities equal job requirements), taken individually, grades outweigh references, extracurricular activities, the school's reputation, etc. Grades are important and their impact can be overridden only by an accumulation of other supporting evidence of performance potential.

When asked about the most important personal qualities sought in an interview, one-third rated self-expression (communicative ability) as the most important quality. About one-fourth viewed expressed goals as most important, and one-fourth viewed personality as most important. Regardless of which is first, when over 80% document these three qualities as the ones most influencing their decisions, it is necessary for applicants to start thinking of how to best rate high in all three areas.

When asked about the importance of grades to future job performance, about one-half saw no direct relationship. In analyzing the responses, it appears that grades are relatively important in the research and development areas (engineering, science, etc.) and less important in nontechnical areas (marketing, etc.). When asked to list the most important factors that would enhance later career performance in the firm, the employers gave the list shown in Figure 5-2. They are listed in order of importance as perceived by the employers. Ambition, grades, related experience, and basic intelligence are the key factors used to evaluate future potential.

This research gives an idea of what interviewers are seeking. By knowing what they are after, one can make a positive presentation that will accentuate assets and minimize liabilities. It is crucial to study results before outlining an oral presentation.

Purpose of the Interview

The first interview with an employer, either on campus or on location, is normally only an initial screening. Applicants can be told "no further interest," but seldom are they hired. Personnel

department staffs conduct these initial screening interviews and then refer applicants to specific department heads who actually make the decision to hire or not hire.

The second interview with the department manager is largely no different than the one with personnel—they simply see fewer candidates. The preparation for that interview differs little. It is possible that the practitioner may ask questions about a specific skill level for a technical field like accounting, data processing, or engineering. In reading this chapter on interviewing techniques and strategy, the principles apply to both interviews.

The initial job interview, whether on campus or at the employer's office, is one of the most important events following graduation from college. The twenty or thirty minutes spent with the interviewer may determine the entire future course of one's life; yet interviewers seem continually amazed at the number of graduates who drift into job interviews without any apparent preparation and only the vaguest idea of what they are going to say. This suggests the attitude of, "Well, here I am. What do you have for me?" And that's often the end of it—in more ways than one.

Interviewers often speak with ten to fifteen job applicants each day so they become quite professional in the role of identifying talent and potential managers. They often undergo extensive training in this business also. Perhaps some empathy with the interviewers' objectives and problems will help in understanding their role and help shape the applicant's behavior in interviewing.

Although there are no established norms for determining what a company's success ratio in interviewing should be, a random sample of 20 interviews on campus for an entry-level assignment might reveal the results shown in Figure 5-3. This implies that an employer must speak with twenty applicants for each hire. Two-thirds of the students turn down the offer. This does not, however, necessarily mean that each

---

Predictors of Success

Ambition and motivation
Grades
Related work experience
Creativity and intelligence
Teamwork capabilities
Initiative and responsibilities
Good personality (outgoing)
Job "fit"
Specific courses
Adaptability
Leadership ability
Ability to communicate
Work habits

Figure 5-2.

**TYPICAL EMPLOYER
INTERVIEW RESULTS**

20 Interviews
16 Turndowns
4 Follow-ups
3 Offers
1 Acceptance

Figure 5-3.

applicant must take seven interviews before receiving an offer. It is hard for employers to improve their batting average (whether above or below that suggested above); but it is relatively *easy* to improve an applicant's success ratio. Following the ideas suggested here will definitely improve the interview. There are many graduates, some with poorer qualifications than others, who receive positive feedback from each interview they take.

This is the most important element of the job search. Success takes hard work. Muffing an interview is easy. By following these suggested ideas, applicants may not get offers from every interview, but it will materially improve their chances to do so.

BEFORE THE INTERVIEW

Get the Facts

This discussion assumes a decision has already been made by the applicant about the type of career of interest, and the sign-up has begun for personal interviews. The first project concerns researching the company of interest. The applicant should try to find out how old the company's products or services are, what its growth has been, and how its prospects look in the future. Also, it would be helpful to know where its plants and offices or stores are located and to what degree the company has established itself as a leader in its field.

SOURCES OF EMPLOYER INFORMATION

Annual Reports
Employment Brochures
Investment Service Publications
Product Brochures
Business Periodicals

Figure 5-4.

This information assures points to discuss in the interview besides the applicant's own interest of finding employment. The interviewer believes in the firm, and expects the applicant to share some of this enthusiasm; and unless the facts are at hand, it is difficult to impress the interviewer of the applicant's interest. It is also quite helpful to try to identify how all of this information relates to the applicant's interests and perceived job duties. Figure 5-1 gives the type of information that one needs prior to each interview.

Answer — Why This Organization?

The applicant should be prepared to answer this question in case the interviewer asks; but more important, it provides an honest answer for one's own thinking. Most candidates trace their interests to the firm's overall reputation, the size of the firm, its location, the type of product or services produced, or the people met through prior dealings with the employer. Perhaps this interest grows from the employer's special opportunities in a field of career interest to the applicant. When the answer to, "What makes this organization different?," is provided by the applicant, a personal interest in the opportunity increases and the applicant's enthusiasm is generally shown.

Arrive Early

It is best to arrive at the interviewing location at least thirty minutes prior to the interview, if possible. Late arrival for a job interview is almost never considered excusable. An early arrival provides the time to recall items about the interview, particularly those points the applicant should emphasize, as well as indicating punctuality and interest in the firm.

Attend to Personal Appearance

There are too many other more important factors to be considered in taking a job interview to labor the points of how to dress and hair length to wear. The best guideline in dress is to come prepared for an interview in an attire appropriate with the type of position for which the applicant is applying. *Clothes might be worn that would be appropriate when on the job.* The length of one's hair may not impress every employer, but neither should it retard progress in seeking a position for which an applicant is well qualified.

Get Psyched Up

Applicants must stress the importance of each interview to themselves before trying to convince an employer they are right for the firm. Anticipating questions and phrasing answers in a well-organized fashion is helpful. The mood will need to be serious, but certainly not tense, although it is normal for many people to be nervous during an interview. Most professional interviewers will certainly overlook initial nervousness. If they are good, they will help smooth the entrance to the interviewing situation by attempting to relax the applicant with questions not really crucial to the interviewing situation.

Getting psyched up for an interview is no different than what a coach of a championship team attempts to do before a big game. Every interview is a major challenge. If not, there is no reason in an applicant wasting the employer's valuable time and taking the time slot from a really interested applicant. The way to face a challenge is to be convinced that the challenge can be met.

Talking to oneself about the importance of the interview can be helpful. Individuals who are convinced they are the best candidate for the opening will be most influential with the interviewer. Applicants must develop confidence in their ability to handle the assignment. Confidence helps develop the psychological state needed. The peak confidence level should coincide with the exact timing of the given interview. Only then is one psychologically prepared and ready to meet the employer.

DURING THE INTERVIEW

Follow the Lead

It will probably be a surprise to learn how fast nervousness disappears after the interview gets underway. Cues can be taken and followed from the recruiter. Greeting the recruiter by name when entering the office is appropriate if the correct pronunciation is known. If not, the applicant should politely ask for the correct pronunciation so that the recruiter's name will be remembered for future reference.

Be Prepared for Questions

Questions may start the minute the interview does. Questions regarding qualifications, career interests, ones that identify personality, and even personal questions can be expected. It is extremely important that applicants be prepared for these ques-

---

NONVERBAL CUES

Nod	Perspiration
Shake head	Posture
Smile	Dress
Laugh	Cologne
Gesture	Jewelry
Smoke	Hair length
Chew gum	Neckwear
Cross legs	Eye contact
Fiddle	Voice tone
Eyebrow	Fingernails
Scratch head	Fidget
Mannerisms	Voice volume
Expressions	Blinking

Figure 5-5.

---

tions so that they are not caught unaware. Figure 5-6 gives a list of "twenty questions" frequently asked by recruiters. The questions are not important. The answers are!

Each question should be reviewed and a brief answer prepared prior to the interview. It is a good idea to answer each of these questions by sitting and watching oneself in a mirror prior to the first interview. This position can give an impression of how to react most favorably. The applicant should try not to answer questions with just "yes" or "no," and talking too much can be just as bad, or worse.

Most interviews will follow a simple question and answer routine. If such is the case, the ability to answer quickly and intelligently is of great importance. If answers seem confused and disorganized, the cause may be lost. The best preventative against a disorganized answer is prior preparation.

An effective technique in answering questions is to use empathy prior to responding. In other words, the applicant should think, "If I were in the recruiter's place, working for the company, what would I like to know about myself?" The answer must, therefore, relate both to the applicant's situation and to the employer's situation, and giving an answer showing the interrelation between the two is most effective. It is often detrimental to learn a speech for each question by rote, but it is necessary to have a number of points in mind prior to the question being asked.

Some form of these questions is likely to be in each interview taken. It helps the applicant to outline responses to each question before the interview. The tricky point is to give the recruiter the answer being sought but to avoid any hint of the answer being contrived and thus having it appear as an insincere response. This potential problem can be minimized by discussing questions and answers with a friend or spouse and requesting an honest critical evaluation. Above all, it is imperative not to lie in a response. Lying about qualifications is easy for an employer to check. Lying about interests is tougher to check, but if the job is taken, and the employee becomes bored and frustrated on the job, the risk of getting fired is high and other employment chances are often hurt.

Accentuate the Positive

Strong points impress employers—they should be emphasized at every appropriate opportunity. All good points should be conveyed to the recruiter because they may not come out unless brought out by the applicant. *Answers must be factual and sincere* without conveying conceit. Being informative without boasting is advantageous to the applicant's cause.

Twenty Frequently Asked Questions

1. Tell me about yourself. Expand on your resume.
2. For what position are you applying?
3. What are your long-term career goals? Where in ten years?
4. Why do you feel that you will be successful in . . .?
5. What supervisory or leadership roles have you held?
6. How do you spend your spare time?
7. What have been your most satisfying and most disappointing experiences?
8. What are your strongest (weakest) personal qualities?
9. Give me some examples that support your stated interest in. . . .
10. Why did you select us to interview with?
11. What courses did you like best? least? why?
12. What did you learn or gain from your part-time and summer job experiences?
13. Which geographic location do you prefer? Why?
14. Would you prefer on-the-job training or a formal program?
15. What can you do for us now? What can I do for you?
16. What are your plans for graduate study?
17. Why did you choose your major?
18. Why are your grades low?
19. Tell me about your extracurricular activities and interests.
20. Why did you quit your various jobs?

Figure 5-6.

Walking this tightrope is difficult, but the success pays handsome dividends. It might be wise to identify one's best qualities in relation to something more tangible. For example, rather than saying, "I am a hard worker and that I want to get ahead," one might say that, "I have worked most of the time that I have been attending college, plus working in the summer, and have taken some extra courses to prepare myself better in my major area of study." The second answer is more effective than the first.

Future Plans

One of the favorite questions of a recruiter, however phrased, concerns employment desires in five or ten years. When this type of question is seen coming, however disguised, it should be remembered that the purpose is to determine ambition, ability to get ahead, and the soundness of one's thinking. The important point is to provide an answer that demonstrates that the applicant has conducted sound thinking in this area. All employers are not looking for the "organization man," but all are looking for ability to succeed in the organization.

Over 50,000 interview ratings of college students at Indiana University have been analyzed. In a large majority of the cases, unsuccessful students were rejected at the initial interview because they had ill-defined career plans. Without discussing the validity of a rejection on that basis, if applicants have not done their homework and if they are not in a position to identify what they wish to do after four years in college, their chances of getting a job in this interview are not good.

Applicants must not convey the impression to the recruiter of not being sure of career direction. Applicants should never say, "I'll do anything if I have the interest and if I'm given a chance to learn," or "I was hoping that perhaps you could identify some areas for which I am qualified." These statements will get a washout about as fast as it takes to make them. Why? First of all, the employers are not job counselors. They have specific jobs to fill or are looking for people in a specific field of work. Their primary objective is to hire people to fill company needs although one may find some professional recruiters giving sound advice. Beware—when recruiters start giving advice they are probably through considering the applicant for a job.

Whenever possible, applicants should apply for a specific job or field of work. Most employers have established, through their literature and other sources, in which fields they have openings. Since the openings are known, the best avenue is to aim for those assignments. The important point is to get into the type of a firm that meets the applicant's established qualifications and one that permits individuals to work hard and show their abilities. After the new employee has succeeded on the initial assignment, different avenues within the firm may open.

If college preparation has not led the student to a specific field of work, it is still unwise, on that account, to pass up chances for interviews. Research in identifying initial starting assignments will better help applicants present their broad qualifications in light of the employer's needs.

Playing Coy

Playing coy is about the best way to burn up employment chances. In each and every interview, applicants should be determined to get the job opening available. Other irons may be in the fire, and professional recruiters will certainly become aware of them the more that is learned of an applicant's qualifications and interests. But before an offer is tendered with a firm, the recruiter must believe that the job is sincerely wanted. Playing the hard-to-get role motivates few employers to increase their efforts to hire an individual; rather, one will find it will turn off most recruiters. Playing coy could materially dim the applicant's chances for an offer.

Asking Questions

As appropriate openings develop in the interview, concrete questions about the company should be asked. It is wise to ask questions that may well have a bearing on whether or not an offer would be accepted if it was extended. Questions that should be avoided are those for which answers could have been obtained by the applicant preparing for the interview. In many cases, the interviewer will have written the employment brochure and surely knows the annual report well, so asking a question that could have already been looked up does not show much industry on the applicant's part.

Questions to ask are those that relate to the type of position for which applying, the geographical location, potential product line growth, etc. Questions should be prefaced with statements that indicate extensive homework about the firm has been done and now additional information is needed. Questions to ask are those that indicate a positive reply is expected from the employer. For example, a statement and question might appear as follows.

> "I noticed that in the job description printed in your employment brochure that all candidates enter into a rather structured program of on-the-job training and classroom instruction. This implies that most new sales representatives are expected to progress at the same pace. With my prior experience in sales, would it be possible to move any faster than two years into a marketing management position?"

In this question, the employer is informed that the applicant has investigated the firm and its training. The thrust of the question assumes that an offer will be forthcoming. It shows ambition. It is a question where the answer may determine whether or not the applicant is interested in pursuing the position further. Every question asked should bring out many facets of the applicant's interests and knowledge of the firm. One should always try to ask "telling question." Figure 5-7 offers some of the typical subjects around which elaborate questions are frequently constructed.

The number of questions asked should not be so many that the interviewer fails to learn enough information about the applicant. The interview should be a mutual proposition. The applicant can do so by showing the appropriate interest. It is wise to have

two or three questions in mind about the company before reporting to the interview. Questions must be pertinent to the subject at hand. If the recruiter or applicant gets on a tangent, they will not be achieving the objectives of the interviewing situation.

Keeping the Faith

After taking a few interviews, identifying the success level of future interviews will develop early in the interviews. If the impression develops that the interview is not going well and that rejection is likely, it is wise, but difficult, to keep enthusiasm high. Nothing is lost by continuing the appearance of confidence and much could be gained. The last few minutes of each interview often change things. Remaining confident and determined will probably make a good impression with the interviewer. Applicants should remember that few employers want to hire individuals who get discouraged easily, particularly in less than a thirty minute interview. Some recruiters even try to discourage applicants to test their tolerance.

If, on the other hand, the recruiter makes it quite evident that the applicant's interests and qualifications emphasized do not match what is available, the applicant should not hesitate to use the situation as a sounding board to help improve future interviews. Most interviewers have a great deal of respect and interest in students or they wouldn't be in their present jobs. Applicants discussing their problems, interests, and ideas with interviewers may benefit from obtaining helpful suggestions. However, the applicant should consider that the interviewer's context may be quite limited and not nearly as broad as that of a professional counselor. All information obtained from employers, counselors, and other placement personnel must be integrated to benefit applicants.

Closing the Conversation

Most interviews last between twenty and thirty minutes. If the interview has been successful, it is possible to reverse this success and talk oneself out of the job. Sum up interests briefly, and express them to the recruiter. As the conversation closes, it is necessary that the applicant understand the next response required. Most recruiters will say that they will be in touch, one way or the other, within three or four weeks.

Some interviewers, however, simply say that if further interests develop they will be in contact within three or four weeks. Therefore, if the applicant does not receive a letter by then, the company is not interested. In some cases, the recruiter will close the conversation by supplying an application form or requesting a transcript. In this case, the next contact must be made by the applicant in letter form to the employer.

Recruiter's Objective

Using some empathy in determining what the recruiter is seeking in the interview is sound advice. The interviewer needs answers to the following questions:

1. Why is the applicant interested in the company?
2. For which position is the applicant applying?
3. What are the applicant's qualifications?
4. How does the applicant compare with others?

If these questions have been answered, the applicant has accomplished a great deal.

State Interest Level

If interest in the position remains, before terminating the interview, the applicant should inform the interviewer of this continued interest. An applicant should thank the interviewer for the opportunity to

---

Frequent Student Inquiries

(Questions are pertinent only if the answer influences you)

How much travel is normally expected?
Do employees normally work many hours of overtime?
Can I progress at my own pace or is it structured?
How frequently do you relocate professional employees?
What is the average age of your first level supervisors?

Is the sales growth in the new product line sustainable?
How much contact and exposure to management is there?
At what level is an employee placed in the "exempt" status?
Is it possible to move through the training program faster?
When does the training program begin? Only in June?

About how many individuals go through your program each year?
What is the housing market for young married couples in. . ?
How much freedom is given and discipline required of the new people?
Would I have to cut my hair and trim my mustache?
Does the firm recommend any night courses the first year?

How often are performance reviews given?
Is it possible to transfer from one division to another?
How much decision-making authority is given after one year?
Have any new product lines been announced recently?
How soon after graduation would I expect to report for work?

How much input does the new person have on geographical location?
In your firm, is this position more analytical or more people oriented?
In promotions, are employers ever transferred between functional fields?
Does the firm provide employee discounts?
Is a car provided to travelling personnel?

Is the city difficult to adjust to compared to this campus community?
What is the average age of top management?
What is the normal routine of a .   .   .   like?
How much independence is allowed in dress and appearance?
Is public transportation adequate?
What is the average time to get to   .   .   .   level in the career path?

THE INITIAL INTERVIEW IS NOT THE TIME TO INQUIRE ABOUT SALARY!

Figure 5-7.

---

discuss their mutual concerns. Ample research proves that first impressions last and here is the last chance to make it a positive impression. Enthusiasm must be clear at this point.

AFTER THE INTERVIEW

Make Notes

After leaving the interviewing room, but before leaving the main office, the applicant should jot down impressions of the interview. It is necessary to get the interviewer's name written and spelled correctly. The interviewer's full title and address should be obtained. Notes should be made of any follow-up that was requested, such as returning an application blank or forwarding a copy of the transcript. Other important information to record include the type of position applied for and some of the major responsibilities and duties of that particular job as it pertains to that employer. Applicants who get an invitation to follow up with further interviews with key executives will be in a position to better recall events that

transpired in the initial interview. If several initial job interviews have been taken and a record of facts is not made immediately following each interview, it is possible to lose track of what was said in the various interviews.

No Answer

If the interviewer seemed interested or indicated further contact and nothing is heard within a reasonable period of time, the applicant should contact the firm. The applicant should wait about two weeks after the indicated contact date before writing a brief letter recalling the conversation. Although thank you letters following interviews are not normally recommended, this could serve as an excellent vehicle to use. The applicant can write a letter of appreciation for the time allotted in the initial interview and briefly express continuing interest. This would also be a good time to include any new information that may have developed and which might have a bearing on employment. At the end of the letter, a comment that a brief note indicating further interest would be appreciated. Little is to be lost at this point in refreshing the interviewer's memory, and it might secure a favorable response. Although it will not help to become a nuisance, it does help applicants to keep their resumes and interests in the foreground in the event that a job requiring the applicant's qualifications does open.

Before becoming too critical of a company and its correspondence record, it is good to remember that a firm recruiter interviews several hundred candidates in a very short period of time. That creates much correspondence and it is easy to get backlogged quickly.

No Interest

If a "nice turndown" (NTD) letter is received, the recipient should not try to read into the letter more than what is there. They are saying simply, "you are not for us but thanks for your time." Some companies, however, do send out letters indicating that they will keep names on file if anything opens up. But this cannot be counted on happening. If an outright turndown is not received and the company indicates that their economic situation may shortly improve or that they may be interested later, there is still a possibility that a job might be landed with them so it is wise to keep in touch. One should not hesitate to begin cultivating this type of potential employer when a small degree of interest is expressed.

In most cases employers will not give a reason as to why they turned down an application. In the majority of cases they have found other candidates whom they feel would be more productive in the assignments that are available. The applicant should not press the company because future interest in the company might develop, either as an employee, a supplier, or a customer.

Keeping in Touch

Graduate school and military bound candidates have some difficulty in getting employers to give them a reply. They may well be interested in the applicant's qualifications, but planning for two or more years in the future may be very difficult in their industry. It would be wise to continue to correspond with such employers advising them of progress made and interest in the firm. Perhaps in graduate school a term paper relevant to their industry could be written and shared with them.

Base Hit

Assuming properly completed homework and a good score on the interviewing exam, it is reasonable to expect a positive reply from an employer. This is a base hit; not a home run. The normal procedure is for employers to extend an invitation to the applicant to visit their facilities for interviewing with people in the stated area of specialization. If there are any expenses to be incurred through the second interview, the employer normally pays them. If this is not completely defined in the invitation letter, this point must be clarified. The home run comes when the firm has successfully interviewed several applicants in the same area of specialization and the manager extends a firm offer in writing.

Problems

Problems will arise throughout the interviewing process, and the best person to answer these questions is the placement director. Many placement offices also have an interviewing feedback process whereby applicants may share in the interview comments about themselves.

Placement officers will not normally identify the comments of specific employers. Even employers expressing continued interest often give considerable criticism hoping that such faults can be corrected before returning for a secondary interview. Employers hesitate to give positive or negative feedback at the time of the interview because they want to see all candidates before making even tentative decisions. If they appear interested and for some reason the position is eliminated or filled by a better candidate, they would be quite embarrassed.

In other words, the placement director can provide some anonymous, constructive criticism. It will only be constructive, however, if use is made of the information that is available. Problems to discuss with the placement director include not hearing from a company or problems of ethics.

SOME STICKY ISSUES

Salary Issue

The salary question is the most frequently discussed issue among students and the most widely misunderstood. In nearly all studies that have been conducted in this area, few students make an employment decision based solely on salary considerations. To be sure, it is important for the salary to be within a general "ball park" range. The overwhelming majority of offers from companies which seek college graduates falls in this competitive salary range.

Although some employers do pay premiums for such items as exceptional grades, previous related work experience, military service completed, and maturity, the differential seems relatively unimportant at the end of one year of work experience with a particular company. It is the job and what goes into it that ultimately determines an employee's salary. Financial success with any employer is usually based entirely on merit, not seniority, and comes as a result of doing an outstanding job in a field.

If the question does occur in an interview situation, the best reply is to state that a salary competitive with others received or anticipate receiving is expected. Placement offices normally publish guidelines regarding the normal range of starting rates for people with a particular type of background. In the majority of cases, employers offer a standard salary for a given assignment for individuals with similar backgrounds. The common reply by an interviewer to the question about salary is normally so general that it is apparent only that they are competitive. In other words, salary should not be discussed in the initial interview unless the subject is forced.

When possessing a significant amount of work experience and an advanced degree, in applying for a job other than an initial starting assignment, it might be wise for the applicant to give the employer some guidelines in regard to the salary range expected. This pertains mainly to individuals with salary requirements substantially above the standard rates who possess the credentials to demand that level of remuneration. Employers may well advise that they are not in a position to offer new employees that remuneration, but there is little value in pursuing dead-end routes by continuing a fake courtship.

Frankness

It is discouraging to answer questions that pertain to lack of success or other limitations. By facing the challenge, without showing disappointment, the applicant welcomes the opportunity to set the record straight. Often a frank admission can be turned to an advantage. For example, an interviewer may ask a question concerning poor grades. It is proper to reply that although overall grades leave much to be desired, more recent grades or grades in a particular major have been significantly higher. This shows the interviewer the applicant's maturity since first entering college. It might also help to identify the extracurricular activities involved in and emphasize any part-time jobs held. The score could be three big pluses with one not-so-embarrassing minus.

For future success it is important that the interviewer identify limitations. It would surely be unwise to place an individual in a situation where poor performance would be likely. Those applicants who are not a Phi Beta Kappa should admit it and point out their strengths. Both the applicant and the employer will be most pleased if the former truly appreciates and candidly discusses weak points.

Personal Questions

Few students seem to enjoy the approach that a number of companies use in identifying potential successful managers. Questions regarding home life, family, friends, and outside activities appear to many students to infringe on their personal privacy. This line of questioning is not very common, but it does occasionally occur so it is helpful to be prepared for it. If such questioning is offensive, the applicant can courteously inform the recruiter that it has no bearing on the qualifications for the job in question. This will convey the message. If not, it is probably not worth sacrificing personal principles to seek employment with that particular firm. It is important to realize, however, that success in any organization whether business, education, or government, may well depend upon factors other than qualifications. In the future when a big job change or promotion is imminent, employees may well find themselves taking a number of personality tests in addition to, in some cases, visiting psychiatrists.

Grades

Nearly all employers state that they wish to hire only candidates in the top half of their graduating class. Each year, however, most graduates, regardless of academic standing, find a career compatible with their qualifications. In other words, few employers hold to their standards as other factors become more overriding than grades alone. Some employers use grades as a crutch to help them identify talented people. They assume that this is the best quantitative measure of a person's ability and initiative. Grades are quite important, but grades alone do not make a qualified individual.

One placement director tells all the employers who recruit on campus that all graduating students are in the upper half of their graduating class. They flunked out the other half!

Students with high grades should not rely on scholarship alone, and students having poor grades should capitalize on other assets. The exceptional students will turn the grade question into a discussion of other activities. This shows interviewers that they have not been spending day and night reading only a textbook, which will help minimize the impression of narrow interests. The student with low grades might well show how other factors such as part-time work experience, class leadership responsibility, social organization activities, sports, hobbies, etc., have contributed to a total education. Such factors as the most recent grades and grades in a major will be considered highly.

Nervousness

With parents, faculty, and counselors emphasizing the importance of getting employment and stressing the interviewing situation, the applicant may become quite tense before the first interview. In fact, a large percentage of students never take an interview on campus simply because they are afraid that they will embarrass themselves or others in their first interview. But waiting until after graduation is generally disastrous if a person wants to go to work for one of the better organizations. Many of the employer's needs will be filled by that time. The first interview is the most difficult. Interviewing becomes much easier after each successive interview until eventually reaching the point of being a routine exercise. Some students become so professional that by the end of the final semester they can go into any interview situation and come out a success.

It is normal to be quite nervous before the first two or three interviews. But this nervousness usually disappears once the graduate is involved in the interviewing situation and the recruiter helps the applicant relax. In many cases, tenseness helps to keep one alert and prepared for circumstances as they develop. It is a good idea to have two or three interviews before taking on the employer who is the number one objective for employment. Confidence will also play an important role in helping overcome nervousness. Adequate preparation breeds the same type of confidence that studying for an exam creates.

HINTS ON IMPROVING PERFORMANCE

Anticipate Questions

Knowing the questions to be asked is only half the problem: the answers are needed also. Applicants who get together with friends and do some role playing will discover how easy first interviews become. Outlining answers to some of the key questions the interviewer is likely to ask also helps. With this outline in mind, the applicant should have a friend ask the "twenty questions" most frequently asked by recruiters. The applicant should practice the answers until it is not necessary to use an outline as a crutch and the ability is developed to respond to questions quickly, concisely, and in a well-organized fashion. Although the recruiter's questions may be worded somewhat differently, they should not be confusing.

Practice Interviewing

Few employers are pleased to find a number of students on their interviewing schedules who signed up to speak to them so that the student can get some interviewing experience for later interviews. An employer comes to campus wanting to locate potential employees and because a number of students have indicated a sincere interest in interviewing with the firm.

INTERVIEW QUESTION TOPICS

Career Objectives—Life Goals

Type of Entry-Level Job

Knowledge of Organization

Personal Qualifications

Reasons for Career Choice

College Preparation

Geographical

Achievements

Activities

Figure 5-8.

Interviewing for information and interviewing for practice has some major disadvantages and should not be tried. Interviewers are most experienced at spotting the phoney and insincere practice interviewer, and they give the student the quality of attention the situation deserves. Some will even challenge applicants with stress interviews or interviews most unrepresentative of what might be expected.

Personnel representatives in a given locale and college recruiters usually know each other well through professional associations and travelling together. It is not uncommon for placement officers to listen to comments over a dinner table about some inconsiderate student with whom the recruiter recently spoke. There is no advantage in incurring the wrath of a recruiter with a job to do (hire qualified talent; not job counsel) who passes negative thoughts about an applicant on to others.

Even if the recruiter is unable to spot a person "just shopping around," that person is still likely to get negative feedback if interest in the firm is not genuine. In the first part of this chapter, the importance of psychological attitude was detailed. Without a high degree of confidence, zeal, and enthusiasm toward the employer and the position, the chances of a successful interview are hampered. If the applicant knows that the interview is just for practice and that no real interest in the firm exists, how can sincere desires for employment be conveyed to someone else?

The only purpose in taking practice interviews is to get some ideas of which approaches work best. Unfortunately, in nearly all cases, all that is likely to be gained is negative feedback—"thanks, but we are not interested." At a period in life when people need positive, not negative feedback, why should they guarantee themselves a negative response through practice or experience interviewing? The first two or three interviews are likely to be rough enough without additional negativism. After the first three interviews, especially after some positive feedback, successive interviews should be relatively easy.

To be sure, the first interviews may not be the most effective. After every interview, even the fiftieth, additional polish of the presentations will occur. Interviewing with an organization in which there is little or no interest does not help. This shows up weak spots in a presentation and insures rejection based upon the interest level displayed. Therefore, the first two or three interviews must be with employers whose job requirements, location, etc., closely meet the applicant's qualifications. The interviews with these employers may not be rated among the five most important, but the results of their outcome should be very meaningful and helpful. Every applicant should go into the first interview with the determination and desire to get a job offer from the employer.

Obtaining interviews in a soft job market may turn out to be as tough as getting a job. Every interview should count. An offer may not be tendered from all of the top five interviews taken, but being successful with number one minimizes rejections.

Specialize

In the overwhelming majority of cases, going into an interview with little idea of what is wanted in the way of a position, will not elicit a favorable response from that interview. Doing so is a waste of time. Once it is known what is available—and it is the applicant's responsibility to find out—there is no advice more sound than to go into the interview and apply for a particular type of job.

Consider the Hypocrite

Even after four or more years of college, many graduates still do not know what type of position they would be most interested in holding. They may have investigated the wide range of entry level assignments and a number of different industries and still come to no firm conclusion. Graduates should pick two or three fields in which an interest exists and talk to employers in these fields; however, it is important in each interview that the type of position for which consideration is desired is specified.

In other words, it is valid for an applicant to tell XYZ Company of an interest in an entry level assignment in sales while ABC is told of an interest in an initial assignment in retail management. If an applicant has an interest in a field and wishes to investigate it, then every effort should be made to land a plant visit or job offer in that field. When considering job offers at a later date, the applicant is then in a position to make a sound decision regarding future career plans.

The logic behind this approach relates to the fact that employers are eager to see an applicant's level of career planning. If little thinking has been done about what one wants to do and why success may be expected in that field, the employer will consider the applicant not worth the risk. An employer is not likely to appraise the interests, personality, values, etc., for the individual and decide (for the applicant) that a certain job in the organization is the best match. Most people seeking employment do not want that either. The employer is looking for a general direction from an applicant and then an explanation of why success in that field can be expected. There-

fore, a tentative decision is better than no decision at all.

In all fairness, this advice to play the hypocrite is not extremely wise, particularly if the two fields selected are unrelated. In the example used above, there are many cross qualifications and similarities between opportunities in sales and retailing. But the commonalities between such fields as marketing and finance often break down. One may be a highly unstructured environment and the other may require a high level of analytical talent and interest in working behind a desk. Few people are capable of being successful on their first job after college to the same degree in different types of jobs. Care in playing the hypocrite is recommended because it can lead to failure later.

Interview—Two-way Street

The interview is a mutual two-way conversation, not a monologue. Applicants need to use their part of the interviewing situation, or they will not be in a position to make some important decisions at a later date. This does not mean that they have to be talking half the time. Listening is as important as talking.

The interviewer's objective is to ascertain the applicant's level of interest, qualifications, and to deliver some information about the employer and opportunities in which an individual might be interested and qualified. It is important to understand and remember what the interviewer says because it could be quite embarrassing at a later date to find the assignment is not what was anticipated. An inability to listen to another person because one is thinking about what to say next is a bad habit.

Stating Views

Some individuals feel that students should parrot exactly what the company wants to hear when they are in the interview situation. There must be an element of give and take in this type of environment. The employer wants to hear the point of view of the student as this is one of the few ways available to evaluate abilities and interests. At the same time that individuals state their views, they must listen to the other person's point of view as well.

Mavericks Allowed

Students may consider that they are not future executive material because they are not willing to fit in a mold that the organization image dictates. All too often, however, stereotype views are automatically assigned without justification. Individuals who feel they are mavericks will be making a great mis-

take when interviewing if they do not let the employer know their true feelings.

Interviewers seldom look for the grey flannel suit as their organization may very well have too many already and they know it. Possessing the intelligence, personality, drive, and the ability to recognize a problem and develop a means for helping solve that problem will be the characteristics possessed by the candidate most interviewers seek. In fact, in looking at top executives of today, many arrived there because they had different ideas along the way with the ability to communicate these ideas to others.

Confidence vs. Cockiness

A thin line exists between the point where confidence turns into cockiness in the interview situation. Being a little overconfident in an interview will probably be more of an asset than a liability; however, prospects should guard against appearing conceited. The difficult thing about the one-to-one interviewing situation may be that applicants who cannot toot their own horn may find no one else to shout their praises.

Rather than running the risk of being a meek, passive, indecisive person in an interview, the best bet is to continue an air of confidence. Start worrying about confidence turning into cockiness only if rejection letters start arriving from employers who previously expressed an interest. In that situation it is advisable to consult the placement officer.

Don't Give Up

Seeking the right career position can be one of the most discouraging events that is ever undertaken. As success begets success, failure generates failure to the point where some students give up. Since the first three interviews are the most difficult, a person should never give up without at least two interviews

above the point of just getting started. Continuing to get rejections after the fifth interview will probably indicate a special problem that should be discussed with a counselor or placement officer.

Most counselors offer feedback advice to students. By asking for feedback when interviewing, a counselor may suggest a change in strategy in the interview situation that may begin a new course of success. It takes time to find the type of opportunity with which some people can be happy. Applicants often reject many employers before they are rejected. There is only one job that can be accepted so it must be one with which the individual can be happy and see a bright future. Giving up means settling for a less desirable choice on one of the most important matters that may affect a person's future happiness.

The average college graduate is likely to take about twenty interviews on campus and another ten off campus before a mutually satisfactory match is made. Interviewing is not simple. *Each* interview should be made into a learning experience. Just as some employees get one year of work experience ten times instead of ten years of experience, some graduates fail to learn from their interview experiences and continue to make the same mistakes over and over and over.

Perseverance is essential but it is not always the solution. As soon as success is below expectations, that is the time to ask for help. It is usually beneficial to review strategy with others, especially the college placement counselor or a faculty member. It may be necessary to rethink self-assessment and its relation to the position(s) for which the applicant is interviewing. Perseverance may be the answer as well.

The Professional Recruiter

Interviewers come in all types of packages, but nearly all have had some training in interviewing prior to being given the responsibility for recruiting. The interviewer on a college campus may be a manager or even president but in most cases has a direct responsibility to the corporate personnel office. Recruiters vary in age from about 27 years to 55 years, and there are good recruiters at all age levels. The ability to communicate effectively with young people is probably the strongest asset that the employer required before sending the recruiter onto a college campus. Professional recruiters know about schools and their programs in addition to what the company has to offer and the positions presently available. Their training will be similar to that described in Figure 5-9.

Empathy with the recruiter's problems is important. Generally speaking, recruiting programs are coordinated through a central corporate office which uses professional staff but occasionally enlists assistance from individuals working in specific fields. For example, if ABC Company had openings only in the sales area, they may send a sales manager to interview. On the other hand, if ABC had a wide range of different types of positions to fill, such as in finance, production, and sales, they may very well send someone from the corporate personnel office. Whoever they send will be trained to handle the initial job interviewing situation.

Although recruiters come in all ages and from a variety of backgrounds, there are certain classifications that some students use to describe the more undesirable recruiters. The "yaker" wants to do most of the talking and judge the applicants' reactions—interest, comprehension, and intelligence—shown in the interview. The "yaker's" evaluation centers around information given on the resume and job application form. This recruiter may be disliked for not giving applicants the opportunity to perform and show their assets not listed on a piece of paper. The applicant may find it necessary to break into the conversation whenever convenient because a decision based on a piece of paper may not be desirable.

Contrastingly, the "deadpan" recruiter hardly speaks at all but merely guides conversations in the direction desired. This may be disappointing because

---

Recruiter's Guide for Successful Interviewing

I. Preparation for the interview (five minutes)

    1. Know the school and its basic program
    2. Know the opportunities available in your company
    3. Read each student's resume prior to the interview

II. The interview (your information—ten minutes)

    1. Warm-up (setting the student at ease)
    2. Obtaining additional information that expands on the resume (abilities and skills)
    3. Ask questions that focus on personality
    4. Ascertain student goals—present and future

III. The interview (student's information—ten minutes)

    1. Relate information on your company
    2. After student identifies the area of interest, explain your programs or openings in his area of interest and competence
    3. Counsel if no interest

IV. Interviewing skills

    1. What data to collect—ability, interests, personality
    2. Interviewing techniques—patterned, non-directive, defensive, etc.
    3. Knockout factors
    4. Showing interest but not committing

V. Evaluation (five minutes)

    1. Complete your evaluation form
    2. Inform the placement office of your evaluation for their counseling program
    3. Make recommendations for further interviews or a rejection

Figure 5-9.

it is difficult to determine what information is being sought. The "deadpan" gives little positive or negative reinforcement during the interview. This approach to the interview forces applicants to sell themselves, and they must call on their knowledge of themselves and their interest in the work being considered to be effective. Preparation prior to the interview will prove to be the greatest asset in providing the information being sought.

Although most interviews follow a typical question and answer routine, the "questioner" rapidly runs through a standard set of questions which must be answered. Since the pace is sometimes hectic, it is difficult for some people to organize their responses. Again, prior preparation is important. Graduates seldom enjoy the structured set of questions so the feedback about the recruiter is often negative. The "human" element seems to be missing. The approach is dictated by the firm so it is unlikely to change. It is necessary to give complete answers, never "yes" or "no," to each question. Interjecting humor into responses, where appropriate, can be an effective method in helping to obtain the desired results.

Knockout Factors

Each time an employer says "no" to an applicant, a basic problem may have motivated the decision. Surprisingly, the same "knockout factors" (Figure 5-10) continue to be prevalent in the majority of rejected applicant situations. When receiving rejections, the natural tendency is to ask "why?" The knockout factors identify the more common reasons. By thoroughly reviewing these with extreme care the applicant can begin to answer the question, "Does that identify me?"

The knockout factors are important because they influence all of the applicant's qualifications for

a given job. It is common to find a major "halo effect" in reviewing an employer's rating. Although appearance may not be as important as the ability to communicate effectively, when a recruiter marks someone low on appearance there is a tendency to rate low on several or all other characteristics. Therefore, it is important to not get trapped into assuming that it is not necessary to worry about a certain problem area simply because other areas for an applicant are strong.

Of course, individuals may get turned down for a given job simply through no fault of their own. Often an employer finds other candidates with overall stronger appearing qualifications. There have been examples also of situations in which the qualifications of two or more candidates are identical and the employer's decision is a toss-up. There is not much that can be done when one is turned down for these reasons except to keep persevering until the toss of the coin is positive.

Interview Evaluation

Each recruiter rates the applicant following the interview. It is helpful to know before the interview on what factors one may be evaluated. Not so surprisingly most recruiters use a similar format regardless of the type of position for which they are interviewing. The "Interview Evaluation Record" shown in Figure 5-11 is an adaptation of forms used by many employers. Figures 5-12 and 5-13 are other types of forms employers often use. One can study all three carefully to understand the criteria used by employers in assessing potential.

An interesting exercise, and one which can provide a meaningful learning experience, is to do a self-rating after each interview. This is done by assuming the recruiter's role and drawing conclusions from that perspective. Thus, when invitations

Figure 5-10.

for secondary interviews are not forthcoming, a record of impressions is available and poor performance areas can be pinpointed so they can be worked on before the next appointment.

SUMMARY

The guides and suggestions presented in this chapter on interviewing techniques are designed to improve chances for the applicant of getting called for further interviews or producing an offer. The problem with giving such interview coaching advice is that if everyone followed the ideas, recruiters could become frustrated since their selection criterion would be more difficult to apply. Everyone would meet them! Some employers just do not see how helpful interview coaching can be to them. Rather than having thousands of unqualified candidates to interview, they would find only a select number of qualified people on their interview schedules because a great number of candidates would screen themselves. The cost of recruiting would decrease and the quality of hires increase.

It is important to remember that strategies presented in this chapter apply equally to the secondary interviews with operating department managers discussed in the next chapter.

Purpose: Career Counseling—Firm Name Is Not Identified to the Student

INTERVIEW RECORD

INDIANA UNIVERSITY   BUSINESS PLACEMENT

CANDIDATE'S NAME	EMPLOYER	INTERVIEWER	DATE

Please Use Check or Comments

CHARACTERISTICS	OUTSTANDING	ABOVE AVERAGE	SATISFACTORY ACCEPTABLE	LIMITED POTENTIAL	NOT ACCEPTABLE
	(A)	(B)	(C)	(D)	(F)
A. APPEARANCE Grooming ☐ Bearing ☐ Posture ☐ Manners ☐ Dress ☐ Neatness ☐					
B. PREPARATION FOR INTERVIEW Knowledge of Company ☐ Knowledge of Positions Open ☐ Asked Pertinent Questions ☐					
C. VERBAL COMMUNICATION Delivery and Animation ☐ Presentation of Ideas ☐ Grammar and Vocabulary ☐					
D. DIRECTION Well-Defined Goals ☐ Confidence in Abilities ☐ Realistic and Practical ☐					
E. MATURITY Responsible ☐ Leader—Campus ☐ Self-Reliant ☐ Judgement ☐ Decisive ☐ Leader—Work ☐					
F. SINCERITY Genuine, Wholesome Attitude ☐ Honest and Sincere ☐ Artificial ☐					
G. PERSONALITY Enthusiastic ☐ Aggressive ☐ Extrovert ☐ Unresponsive ☐ Motivation ☐ Noncommittal ☐					
H. QUALIFICATIONS Academic Preparation ☐ Work Experience ☐ Position Match ☐					
I. OVERALL EVALUATION Long-Range Potential ☐ Drive and Ambition ☐ Ability and Qualification ☐					

SCALE BASE = COMPANY HIRING STANDARDS

Strong Points Sour Notes Advice Hiring Problems Background Amplify Above Suggestions Plans Personal Hints	CANDID COMMENTS PLEASE! EXTREMELY HELPFUL! !

PROBABLE ACTION

☐ Invitation   ☐ No Job Match   ☐ Uncertain at This Time

☐ Offer   ☐ No Mutual Interest   ☐ Will Refer to _____

Candidate Will Be Contacted by What Date? _____

Return to PLACEMENT ASSISTANT at end of day. Thank you for the help given this student.

Figure 5-11.

SELECTION AND EVALUATION SUMMARY

Applicant's Name _____ Date _____ 19 ____

Position Applied for _____

	RATING ON EACH FACTOR	Out-standing	Good	Mar-ginal	Poor
"CAN DO" FACTORS	Appearance, manners				
	Availability for this work				
	Education as required by this job				
	Intelligence, ability to learn, solve problems				
	Experience in this field				
	Knowledge of the product				
	Physical condition, health, energy				

	CHARACTER TRAITS (BASIC HABITS)				
"WILL DO" FACTORS	Stability; maintaining same jobs and interests				
	Industry; willingness to work				
	Perseverance; finishing what he starts . .				
	Ability to get along with people				
	Loyalty; identifying with employer				
	Self-reliance; standing on own feet, making own decisions				
	Leadership				

MOTIVATION				
Interest in this work				
Economic need				
Need for recognition				
Need to excel				
Need to serve				
Need to acquire				

DEGREE OF EMOTIONAL MATURITY				
Freedom from dependence				
Regard for consequences				
Capacity for self-discipline				
Freedom from selfishness				
Freedom from show-off tendencies				
Freedom from pleasure-mindedness				
Freedom from destructive tendencies . . .				
Freedom from wishful thinking				

<u>Important</u>: Do not add or average these factors in making the over-all rating. Match the qualifications of the applicant against the requirements of the particular position for which the individual is being considered.

Strong points for this position _____

_____

Weak points for this position _____

_____

Over-all Rating: ☐A ☐B ☐C ☐D   Recommendation to employ: ☐ Yes ☐ No   Rating by _____

Figure 5-12.

INTERVIEW REPORT

NAME OF APPLICANT _____

DATE OF INTERVIEW _____

APPLYING FOR _____

INTERVIEWER_____

Please Report Your Interview Impressions By Checking the One Most Appropriate Box in Each Area

1. APPEARANCE: very untidy; poor taste in clothes	Somewhat careless about personal appearance	Satisfactory personal appearance	Good taste in clothes; better than average appearance	Unusually well groomed; very neat; excellent taste
2. FRIENDLINESS: appears very distant and aloof; cool	Approachable; fairly friendly	Warm; friendly; sociable	Very sociable and outgoing	Extremely friendly and sociable
3. POISE, STABILITY: ill at ease; "jumpy"; appears nervous	Tense; easily irritated	About as poised as the average applicant	Sure of himself	Extremely well composed; probably calm under pressure
4. PERSONALITY: unsatisfactory for the job	Questionable for this job	Satisfactory for this job	Very desirable for this job	Outstanding for this job
5. CONVERSATIONAL ABILITY: talks very little; expression poor	Makes attempts at expression; fair job at best	Average fluency and expression	Talks well and to the point	Excellent expression; extremely fluent; forceful
6. ALERTNESS: slow to catch on	Rather slow; requires more than average explanation	Grasps ideas with average ability	Quick to understand; perceives very well	Exceptionally keen and alert
7. INFORMATION: poor knowledge of field of interest	Fair knowledge of field of interest	Is as informed as the average applicant	Fairly well informed; knows more than average applicant	Has excellent knowledge of the field
8. EXPERIENCE: no relationship between applicant's background and job requirements	Fair relationship between applicant's background and job requirements	Average amount of meaningful background and experience	Background very good; considerable experience	Excellent background and experience
9. DRIVE: has poorly defined goals and appears to act without purpose	Appears to set goals too low and to put forth little effort to achieve these	Appears to have average goals; puts forth average effort to reach these	Appears to strive hard; has high desire to achieve	Appears to set high goals and to strive incessantly to achieve these
10. TEST RESULTS: too low to be considered	Substandard but possibly acceptable	Average	Above average and shows potential	Outstanding

ELIGIBLE FOR EMPLOYMENT: YES_____ NO_____ _____

                                          SIGNATURE OF INTERVIEWER

Figure 5-13.

6

COMMUNICATIONS:
Letters—Forms—Ethics

The applicant evaluative process does not end after the initial interview whether it is on campus or at the employer's facilities. A long sequence of written communications is only beginning for candidates seeking a professional assignment. The initial interview with the personnel manager is normally followed by further interviews at the employer's facilities.

The secondary interview initiates a series of further interviews with a number of different people employed in the department that has the actual job opening. Most employment decisions result only after a number of people discuss opinions about the potential employee. Rarely will one person assume total responsibility for hiring. The secondary interview is often referred to as the plant visit or office visit.

If the initial interview is at the employer's facilities, the secondary interview may be conducted the same day. The current trend is for the personnel manager to request that the applicant return at a later date. The purpose of a later visit is to insure that all of the appropriate decision makers are available.

After the initial interview most employers contact applicants by telephone or letter requesting some specific dates which are mutually satisfactory. Although many employers send the nice turndown letter to applicants in whom they have no further interest, some employers do not reply to applicants

turned down. As a general rule, if the employer does not contact applicants within six weeks, little possibility for further consideration exists.

The positive contact from the employer prompts a detailed sequence of letters, applications, expense forms, and other paperwork. Correspondence takes time. Even though a candidate is simultaneously interviewing other employers, visiting others, studying, taking exams, and trying to maintain a social life, attendance to correspondence etiquette is imperative. One disgusted employer can blackball an applicant's chances with many other employers. A close working relationship between employers, particularly campus recruiters, is very common.

The list of employment communications given in Figure 6-1 gives an appreciation of the scope and magnitude of the problem. As three or more invitations develop, work builds up rapidly. Since all avenues of employment have to be conducted simultaneously, it is not possible to follow one sequence through before responding to others.

Students near the top of the graduating class seldom schedule more than five overnight office visits per semester even though many more employers may want to see them. It is not possible to do much more and still maintain a respectable academic record. A normal trip takes two study nights and a day and a half of class periods. Because of this, the top students

should plan to limit on-campus interviews to a reasonable number in order to give other students a crack at the secondary interview process.

The time consuming communication process can be moderated considerably by an advance plan of action. It is far more important to prepare for secondary interviews than to spend time struggling with letter writing and yet the letter writing is equally important.

All employers use a standardized set of correspondence and form letters for the purpose of contacting job applicants. Only minor changes are made in each letter when it is sent to applicants.

Job candidates may also own a set of form letters to use in corresponding with potential employers. Of course, letters must be modified each time to

fit individual circumstances, but basic construction may change little.

REQUIRED CORRESPONDENCE

The end of this chapter contains a set of letters that may be used in contacting employers. The letters, however, represent only a small part of the total communication process. It is important to understand the total communication from the perspective of interviews, itineraries, and employment communications.

Interview Evaluation

The sequence of communication actually begins with the resume and cover letter discussed in Chapter 4. The initial interview is followed by an interview evaluation which serves as a record for the applicant. Many effective job campaigns require over thirty interviews both on and off campus. Few candidates can remember the items discussed and the appropriate follow-up without some written record.

If the response after the interview is positive, the evaluation serves very useful in planning for future interviews. If the response is negative, the evaluation serves to help the candidate figure out what went wrong. Evaluations should be kept on all interviews—initial and secondary. A sample format is given at the end of this chapter.

Letter Style

Business letter writing style is seldom taught in college, and few students gain any experience in this form of communication. A universal format, style, and etiquette is accepted and used by nearly all organizations. It is so elementary that it seems hardly worthwhile to discuss the mechanics, but each year a large number of job candidates alienate potential

---

EMPLOYMENT COMMUNICATIONS

Resume
Cover Letter
Thank You
Application
Accepting Invitation
Declining Invitation
Thank You for Visit
Expense Statements
Terminating Discussions
Offer Acknowledgment
Offer Stall
Offer Acceptance
Offer Declination
Keep in Touch (nudge)
Notes on Interview

Figure 6-1.

employers simply because they do not use the business writing style. Professional communication ability remains a significant factor that employers use in evaluating and comparing applicants.

Figure 6-2 shows the style of a typical business letter. The blocking and spacing may vary slightly. Most college graduates, regardless of position title, write hundreds of similar styled letters during their career. Although interorganization memos vary somewhat, the primary thrust is very similar.

A sample copy of every reply written by job applicants to employers is given at the end of this chapter. Each letter must be individually typed and as error free as the resume. Ideally, a letter should be written after each telephone call or received letter to confirm your understanding of the situation but time pressures often curtail this. Most misunderstandings occur because of the failure to follow up in writing. The employment topic is one that affects a person's entire working career, so attention to details is truly worth the small amount of extra time.

Always keep a copy of every letter sent. It will save later embarrassment. Given the mail service and lack of service, showing an irritated potential employer the copy may save a job offer. Even better insurance is to send a copy of every letter that you write to your college placement office.

Most college placement offices maintain a file on each graduating student. In due process the files are open for inspection by job applicants. Frequently employers call the placement officer just before making an offer or to complain about the lack of common courtesy by a student. Placement officers invariably pull the file so they can see the true chain of events. Most major employers also send copies of all correspondence to students to the placement office. The placement office can often assist students who have had mail difficulties by showing students copies of letters they should have received from employers. Graduates should also maintain their own personal correspondence file by employer.

The importance of proper communication cannot be overemphasized. Written communication is the backbone of every personnel office. A positive chain of communication shows the employer that the applicant sincerely wants the job. A high level of interest frequently swings the positive decision even though another candidate may have a slightly stronger record.

Thank You

A thank you letter after every initial interview is not necessary but in certain instances where interest is very high, it is appropriate to send a follow-up. A thank you letter simply restates a high level of interest in a career with the organization.

In some instances, thank you letters can serve another purpose. Some employers fail to respond expeditiously to job candidates and need a nudge. The "nudge" letter is sent under the guise of a thank you about six to eight weeks after the initial interview. A polite way to remind the employer is to enclose an updated resume or to comment about any new developments since the initial interview. Another approach is to say that graduation is approaching, and a decision is necessary but that the decision can be postponed until a reply, one way or another, is received from the number one choice.

Application Forms

Every employer demands completion of the organization's official application blank. Even if the resume contains the exact same information, an application is required for legal, data processing, and employer convenience reasons.

The College Placement Council has a tacit agreement with most major employers that a completed application before the on-campus interview is not necessary if the student has completed the standardized "College Interview Resume" used by the placement office from a format adopted and approved by the Council. If there is any further interest in the applicant after the campus interview, an application is required.

The application is an official document. The information must be complete and accurate. If the blanks are inadequate for a certain situation, explain it on an attached page.

The application often follows employees for years. Career progress decisions are made on the basis of information contained in applications which may be several years old. Employers tend to update applications by placing new career and salary progress and appraisals into the employee's personnel file. Thus, a well-completed initial application is in the applicant's best interest.

Everyone enjoys reading a document that is neat, error and smudge free, typed, centered, and complete. Typing application blanks is not always possible, but if time is available, one should do it. The form often is copied and circulated widely internally, and a typed form makes a more pleasant representation.

If one has no significant work experience related to the entry-level assignment, the salary desired blank may be left open. For candidates with work experience and/or a minimum acceptable salary, the minimum should be specified. If the employer cannot

```
                                        Street Address
                                        City, State, Zip
                                        Current date

           (4 spaces)

Employer's Name
Title
Department
Organization
Street Address
City, State, Zip
           (1 space)
Dear Mr./Ms./Dr./individual's name:
           (1 space)
Introduction: Reference previous conversation or corre-
spondence . . . give specific dates if possible . . .
state appreciation for past consideration . . . suc-
cinctly state current business.
           (1 space)
Body: Give details on purpose of letter . . . make ref-
erence to attachments . . . write short but complete
sentences . . . avoid large and unnecessary words . . .
cover the central theme completely . . . make paragraphs
two to five sentences.
           (1 space)
Close: State the action you expect from the recipient . . .
keep paragraph short . . . indicate your next plan of
action . . . offer specific date of expected action if
appropriate . . . thank the recipient.
           (1 space)
Very truly yours, (sincerely, sincerely yours, truly yours,
etc.)


           (3 spaces)

Typed Name
           (1 space)
P.S.   Information that came after the letter was written.
       Sometimes used for emphasis.
           (1 space)
Encl. (Indicates that there is an attachment)
           (1 space)
cc Placement Office (Indicates others who are kept informed)
```

Figure 6-2.

meet the minimum, an offer is unlikely, so both parties will save much time. Almost no employers negotiate on entry-level salaries, and attempts to do so most often are met with offer withdrawals.

Accepting Invitation

After expressing appreciation for the opportunity to visit the employer's facilities and the further interest, the applicant should suggest three convenient dates in most preferable order for the visit. The acceptance letter should be written even if it is only a formality to confirm the dates agreed upon by telephone. It is an embarrassing situation for both the employer and candidate to arrive and have no itinerary arranged.

The applicant should confirm with the employer whether overnight accommodations are necessary. If yes, it is best to request that the employer make hotel reservations nearby. Advising the employer of your travel plans and time of arrival is standard courtesy.

Not all employers pay expenses for the secondary interview although many do pay. Be prepared to assume the total cost. The applicant may call the employer if there are any doubts as to the cost arrangement. Telephone calls should not be made collect unless advised to do so. The employer must be notified immediately if changes occur or last-minute emergencies develop. The employer has likely developed a schedule of executives who must interview the applicant.

Declining Invitation

Once it has been decided that interests are elsewhere, the candidate should thank the employer for the consideration that has been displayed and state that other career plans have been made. Never ignore an invitation letter. A response one way or another is essential within three to five days.

Reaffirming Interest

After the visit to the employer's offices, a brief note indicating continued interest should be sent. The expense statement is usually attached and other details of the visit discussed. The letter should always express thanks and appreciation.

Expense Statements

Many times the employer will request an expense voucher before reimbursing expense money. This could be included in the letter reaffirming interest. In most cases, the employer refunds expenses at the end of the day of the visit. If the employer does not provide a form to complete, the one given in this chapter is acceptable. Candidates should be careful to remember that not all employers pay expenses.

Some employers recognize that students do not have a great deal of cash lying around and make provisions to provide a cash advance upon request. Some universities also maintain revolving loan funds for short-term loans for students traveling. The sums needed can be significant and create major cash flow problems.

Few students spend less than $20,000 for a degree if they do not live at home. An effective job campaign can easily cost $500 to $2,000 including resumes, letters, travel, and moving expenses. It is an expenditure that should be planned in advance.

Never pad an expense account. Employers pay expenses day in and day out and know what reasonable costs should be. A blackballing letter from an employer to a placement office is extremely damaging.

Terminating Discussions

If after the visit it is determined by the candidate that no interest exists in pursuing employment further, the employer should be so advised. The employer should be thanked for the consideration shown and the candidate can state that other plans have been made. This should be done as soon as the decision is made so the employer can extend an offer to someone else.

Offer Acknowledgment

After receiving an offer, written or verbal, an immediate acknowledgment of the offer should be made. The employer should be thanked for the interest shown and an understanding of the terms discussed (salary, job title, duties, etc.) repeated.

The employer is aware that a candidate may have other irons in the fire; it is proper, therefore, to indicate the date on which a decision will be made. If that date rolls around and more time is needed, an extension can be requested. It must be remembered, however, that an employer has the right to withdraw the offer any time prior to acceptance.

Some employers extend more offers than job openings available, and when enough students accept, they withdraw those offers still outstanding. However, most employers will hold an offer open until the date mutually agreed upon. Whenever any questions arise, the college placement officer is the appropriate person to contact.

Acceptance of an Offer

This letter constitutes a moral contract between the candidate and the employer. An acceptance should again include the terms as they are understood. Also, such items as physical examination, if required, reporting date, and perhaps home hunting plans should be discussed. Incidentally, almost no employers pay moving expenses for entry-level jobs.

Only one job offer can be accepted! The decision is a binding commitment. If a more attractive offer comes at a later time, it must be rejected on ethical grounds. The decision to accept should not be taken lightly or done in haste. If undue pressure to make a decision is exerted by a given employer, it would be wise to contact the placement officer. In the final analysis, the decision to accept or reject an offer within a few weeks is up to the candidate.

It is seldom possible to collect all potential offers and then to make a decision after they are all in. Both students and employers must make decisions in a chronological sequence. When one student turns down an offer, the employer must have enough time left to extend the offer to another applicant. Obviously, employers cannot wait much longer than six weeks before graduation for a decision. All other good graduates will be placed by then.

The penalty for an unethical practice can be severe. The rejected employer normally writes or calls the placement office and requests a note of complaint be registered with the College Placement Council and the circumstances placed in the student's file. The current employer is often advised of the circumstances and can fire the new employee. An honest statement of the circumstances could also be placed in the individual's retail credit file as a comment on character. In short, reneging on offers is not worth the long-term risk.

Rejection of an Offer

As soon as a decision on accepting a job is made, it is important to immediately notify all other employers of that fact. The candidate should simply advise them that this was a difficult decision but that this employer's opportunities fit better in line with held interests and aspirations.

It is proper to indicate where employment was accepted, but it is not necessary. By courteously

---

UNETHICAL EMPLOYMENT PRACTICES
Inaccurate resume
Falsifying records
Incomplete records
Dishonest recommendations
Lying in interviews
Cheating on expenses
Insincere job interest
Abusing confidentiality
Reneging on acceptance
Leaving job prematurely

Figure 6-3.

POTENTIAL SANCTIONS FOR UNETHICAL CONDUCT
Prepare report of situation
Note in placement file
Notify current employer
Advise potential employers
Inform credit agencies
Consult references
Advise Placement Council
Inform employment agencies
Contact personnel associations

Figure 6-4.

thanking them for their interest the candidate may keep the doors open for the future.

Few things irk placement officers more than seeing a student collect job offers as if he/she were on a major ego trip. The placement officer is responsible for placing everyone in the class, not just the top four or five graduates. Offers collected by top students take away from offers that likely would have been extended to other students. Realistic evaluation of more than five offers is not possible.

The offer ego trip hurts employers because the accept ratio must be low. The ego trip hurts other students because few employers extend more than a given number of offers to students at any one school. The ego trip adds nothing of a constructive nature to an applicant's long-term career objectives.

Everyone can be helped by encouraging students to reject offers as soon as possible if no further interest is warranted. Employers can meet manpower plans by extending an offer to another student at that school. Other students find employment.

THE SECONDARY INTERVIEW

Before preparing for the visit, an understanding of what to expect after arriving plays a key role in the ability to communicate well. A state of confusion leads nowhere. Each situation may need to be handled differently, but a pattern may be expected from each employer.

Flexibility in the itinerary is a standard procedure. As campus interviews vary from interviewer to interviewer, so will the visit, although in contrast to speaking with a single campus interviewer, several interviewers will be seen.

Upon arrival, the candidate usually reports to the personnel department as this department normally has the responsibility for plans for the day.

The individual to whom reporting may or may not be the interviewer met previously. Personnel's role normally is designed as a liaison and, therefore, the following points may be discussed:

1. The outline for the day's activities.
2. Company organization.
3. General employment procedures and guidelines.
4. Answers to general questions.

One of the most important reasons for extending an invitation is to introduce a candidate to managers and employers in the field of interest. It is reasonable to expect to be interviewed by four to eight individuals, most of whom will be working in the area of specialization or interest. They will evaluate abilities, competence, and personality. These interviews are quite similar to campus interviews, only there are more of them.

Many of these interviews are carbon copies of each other. The employer wants to expose the candidate to a wide array of people, all of whom will be evaluating the candidate. It is important to not let down in any of them because one "no interest" can ruin chances for employment. Giving the same presentation over and over can become boring but boredom should not be shown.

Most interview visits begin at 9:00 A.M. and continue until 5:00 P.M. Some firms will pick the candidates up before 8:00 A.M. and deliver them to the airport in the evening. Little, if any, free time can be expected as even lunch is reserved for interviews.

Many employers administer psychological tests even during one-day visits. Tests may last from one-half to three hours. There is a trend, however, of many employers shortening or eliminating testing programs.

A survey of 196 companies in 1973 by the Endicott Report indicated that 25% of the enployers recruiting college graduates used some type of testing program for selection purposes. Almost half of the firms using tests administered fewer types of tests than in recent years so the trend appears to be away from a significant use of tests for selection.

Tours of the employer's facilities are not uncommon although it is not always a standard procedure. If it is not and an interest exists, it is proper to ask about it.

Near the end of the interviews, the liaison person will again be met. The candidate may be requested to express impressions of the day and in return can expect some feedback on progress accomplished. Many of the interviewers will have returned their impressions.

In many cases, an intuitive idea of how the interviewing is progressing will develop. However, the candidate should not plan on receiving an offer at this time. If a verbal offer is extended or the employer implies that an offer is likely, the candidate can expect to receive it in writing in two to four weeks.

If expenses have not been mentioned by the end of the day, the candidate should ask what procedure should be followed for reimbursement. Many employers refund expenses at the end of the day while others request an expense statement. Nearly all require receipts, so they should all be saved and given to the employer at the appropriate time.

If visiting other employers on the same trip it is necessary to prorate expenses. Besides the ethics involved, personnel people seem to have a close local fraternity and knowledge of excellent candidates rapidly spreads, so a person can jeopardize employment chances by fudging on an expense statement.

SUMMARY

This concludes the mechanics of the communication process and secondary interview. These interviews determine whether or not the job offer is tendered and as such are equally as important as the initial interview. Preparation, as always, is crucial. Before the visit, it would be wise for candidates to review the chapter on interviewing and rehearse the interview presentation.

CONTACT IMPRESSION EVALUATION

Company name_____ Date_____

Individual contacted_____

    Address:

Position applied for_____

How initial contact was made: Campus Interview_____Letter_____

    Other_____

Comments on First Contact

Probable action by recruiter:

    No interest _____ Uncertain_____Is interested_____

Follow Up Procedures

Who will initiate next contact? They_____Me _____

Date by which contact should be made _____

Nature of contact:

Actual date of follow up contact_____

Nature of follow up message: _____

Date consideration terminated_____

Reason consideration terminated (if self-initiated):

Figure 6-5.

ACCEPTING INVITATION

Your Address
City, State, Zip
Telephone Number
Date

Employer Name
Title
Department
Organization
Address
City, State, Zip

Dear Mr. Employer:

Thank you for your telephone call (letter, verbal offer, etc.) on March 1, 19XX, inviting me to Anywhere, U.S.A., for further interviews. I was pleased to hear from you because after our initial conversation, I was impressed with XYZ's training approach and wanted to be considered further.

I am eager to get together as soon as possible because I hope to make an employment decision around April 1. Since the campus spring break falls between March 11 and 15, would it be possible to get together then? Would March 15 be okay with you? (Or if just confirming, indicate that you plan to arrive by 9:00 a.m. on March 15.)

I prefer to make my own travel plans. Being unfamiliar with your location in Anywhere, would you please make a hotel reservation for two people as my spouse wishes to look around Anywhere. Of course, I will pay any cost over one person. Please advise me of the hotel accommodations.

Your program appears to be exactly what I am seeking. I will arrive in your office by 9:00 a.m. unless advised otherwise. Thank you for your consideration.

Very truly yours,

(Sign and type your name)

P.S. Enclosed is your completed application blank. A transcript is also enclosed.

cc: Placement Office

Figure 6-6.

REAFFIRMING INTEREST

Address
City, State, Zip
Telephone
Date

Mr. Employer Name
Title
Department
Organization
Address
City, State, Zip

Dear Mr. Employer:

Thank you for arranging a most complete day of interviews for me last week. Because of a well-planned and organized day of interviews with so many people the day seemed to fly by. I hope that your people were as impressed with me as I was with them. I can see why you are so profitable with such a high caliber management staff.

Enclosed is the expense statement which you requested. The hotel apparently billed directly to you because the desk clerk said there was no charge when I checked out.

The visit was truly an enjoyable and productive day for me. I am even more enthused about pursuing employment further with you. I have enclosed a copy of a recommendation letter from a former employer which you may include in my file. In my interview with Mr. Smith, he expressed some reservation about my writing and research ability, so I am also enclosing a copy of a term paper showing my capabilities. (Any additional information you may wish to use to support your cause should be included but don't overdo it.)

I am anxiously awaiting your reply. Of all the employers I have interviewed, your opportunity is one of the most exciting to me. If you require any additional information, please call me.

Very truly yours,

(Sign and type your name)

cc: Placement Office
Encls.

Figure 6-7.

INTERVIEW TRIP EXPENSE REPORT

Name_____

Address_____

City, State, Zip_____

Telephone_____

Date of Visit_____

Transportation

    From Home to Airport   _____

    Airline Fare (Receipt Attached)   _____

    From Airport to Home   _____

    Taxi/Limousine Fares   _____

    _____   _____

    _____   _____   _____

Lodging

    Hotel ( ) (Receipt Attached) _____

    Hotel Tips   _____

    _____   _____   _____

Meals

    Meals Prior to Interview   _____

    Meals Enroute Home   _____

    _____   _____   _____

TOTAL EXPENSES INCURRED   _____

Signature_____Date_____

Figure 6-8.

ACKNOWLEDGING OFFER

> Your Address
> City, State, Zip
> Telephone
> Date

Employer Name
Title
Department
Organization
Address
City, State, Zip

Dear Mr. Employer:

Thank you for your telephone call on March 1 offering me a position as a _____ in your _____ department at an annual salary of $ _____. You cannot imagine the joy with which I received your call. After my visit, I left saying to myself that you are the type of organization with which I can be proud to be a part. I was truly impressed with all of the people to whom I spoke.

I understand that you must have a decision within three weeks and I will call or write you before then.

This is exactly the type of challenge and opportunity that I am seeking. I am pleased that you have put forth such confidence in me. If you need additional information, please call me. Thank you for your consideration.

Very truly yours,

(Sign and type your name)

cc: Placement Office

Figure 6-9.

ACCEPTING OFFER

Address
City, State, Zip
Telephone
Date

Employer Name
Title
Department
Organization
City, State, Zip

Dear Mr. Employer:

Thank you for all of the time that you have spent considering me for a position as a _____ in your
_____ department. I am very appreciative of your efforts and those of Mr. _____
and Mr. _____ who have given so much of their time.

I have just made one of the most difficult decisions of my life. With which organization should I begin my career?
I have been fortunate in having a choice between several of the most outstanding opportunities and challenges ever
presented to me. Last week I narrowed my choice to two employers of which you were one.

I wish to accept your offer as a _____ in your _____ department at the salary of
$ _____. I recognize that this is contingent upon my passing a routine physical examination from
which I anticipate no difficulty. The influence of Mr. _____ triggered my decision because I think
that it will be a pleasure to work with him. I thrive under people who present challenges and have his knack of
making one want to do the job.

I wish to report for work as soon after graduation, May 15, as possible. Please let me know an acceptable starting date. My wife and I plan to take Ms. _____ up on her offer to help us search for an apartment
which we hope to do about two weeks before my starting date.

Please advise me if there is any other data you need or if any other details need to be handled. Please call any
day after 4:00 p.m. I am eagerly preparing for my new assignment and look forward to talking with you soon.

Very truly yours,

(Sign and type your name)

cc: Placement Office

Figure 6-10.

DECLINING OFFER OR INVITATION

Address
City, State, Zip
Telephone
Date

Employer Name
Title
Department
Organization
City, State, Zip

Dear Mr. Employer:

Thank you for all of the time that you have spent considering me for a position as a _____ in your _____ department. I am very much appreciative of all of your efforts and those of Mr. _____ and Mr. _____ who have given so much of their time to me.

I have just made one of the most difficult decisions of my life. Who should I go to work for? I have been quite fortunate in having a choice between some of the most outstanding opportunities ever presented to me. I narrowed my decision to two employers last week of which you were one. I wish I could accept both.

After much deliberation with my wife, friends, faculty and placement office personnel, I must respectfully decline your invitation to join your _____ department. I feel that another opportunity matches my qualifications and interests better at this stage in my career. In the unlikely event that the other opportunity does not work out as planned, I would hope that you could leave the door open for possible discussions of something else in two or three years. I am very impressed with your operation and professional way of doing things.

After several years in college, I am ready to energetically meet the world of work. I have advised a number of my friends of your cordial and candid approach to hiring college graduates. A number have expressed an interest in speaking with you when they graduate. I know that you have other offers extended to graduates of University and I wish you much success in your recruitment efforts. I sincerely appreciate all of your kindness and consideration toward me.

Very truly yours,

(Sign and type your name)

cc: Placement Office

Figure 6-11.

7

CAREER PROGRESSION:
Decisions—Performance—Education

Assuming that interviewing efforts have produced handsome dividends, and several job offers are in hand, the candidate is now faced with the task of deciding which offer to accept. How does one choose between offers that provide relatively equal starting salaries and excellent advancement opportunities?

It is a delightful position, but the choice is not simple. Making the choice can change the candidates' direction of life-style and move them into a career field that is likely to exist for a lifetime. The initial job decision can influence a career direction and success for years to come. The challenge must not be taken lightly!

THE INITIAL EMPLOYMENT DECISION

How does one make such a decision? From a thirty minute conversation and a one day visit, a wealth of data and facts are not available from which to draw conclusions. But with this limited information and other research data, hopefully, a decision can be found. Recommendations and ideas from faculty, placement officers, friends, parents, etc., are additional aids. Collating even this limited information is a big project especially when considering the impact of the results on the immediate future.

Factors to Consider

A number of studies conducted by researchers quizzing college graduates on why they accepted the position they did provides some help. The rank order varies in these studies depending on the population used. There are differences in rankings based on sex, race, class standing, and academic majors such as engineering, business, liberal arts, etc. Our recent study categorized by sex is given in Figure 7-1.

Whenever an individual is asked to rank factors influencing job choice, the ranking seldom coincides precisely with views of large surveys. Ironically, the top five factors tend to be the same and the next five factors also seldom deviate out of that group of five. Salary consistently falls into the six to ten ranks for most populations quizzed.

Most individuals prefer to develop their own ranking scheme depending upon their personal value structure.

Job Comparisons

One purpose of ranking values is to help quantify the decision to accept one job over others. Few individuals select the first choice that comes along and have a variety of options. An objective scheme to quantitatively rank various choices aids in the final decision. One useful scheme is shown in Figure 7-2.

The job comparison form in no way dictates which employer to select. It is impossible to quantitatively rank all factors because one or two factors may be overriding. Some materialistically oriented graduates may place salary so high on their list that other factors become inoperable. In addition, the qualitative approach offers little help to the person who has offers in several different cities but who, for one reason or another, must locate in a given city. Subjective factors greatly influence job choice.

RANKING OF JOB VALUES INFLUENCING JOB CHOICE

Job Factor	Men	Women
Opportunity for Advancement	1	4
Challenge and Responsibility	2	1
Opportunity for Self-development	3	1
Type of Work	4	5
Freedom on the Job	5	7
Salary	6	6
Working with People	7	3
Job Security	8	8
Training	9	11
Company Reputation	10	13
Fringe Benefits	11	12
Working Conditions	12	10
Location of Work	13	9
Job Title	14	14

Source: *Journal of College Placement,* Winter, 1975.

Figure 7-1.

Cost of Living Comparisons

Such factors as opportunity for advancement, type of position available, company personnel, type of training program, etc., must be given a high priority before making a job decision. Graduates are also concerned about starting salaries and how they compare in different geographical locations.

At first glance, salaries seem much easier to compare than the subjective factors in Figure 7-2. But those who have researched the areas know that a true comparison of starting salaries requires investigation of cost of living indexes, bonus or commission plans, and any special company benefits (such as company car for full-time use, purchase of company products at discount, profit sharing, or low home mortgage financing).

A key item in comparing salary "value" is the *Cost of Living Index* in the cities for which job offers have been received. There is a big difference between costs in Dallas and New York City. How can the candidate quantify this difference? Cost of living comparisons are available and helpful but can be misleading and must be used *with care.* The market basket used in calculating the index may be inappropriate for a single recent college graduate with no dependents. Discrepancies result from the time at which the survey was made, type of survey, family status considered, and whether apartment renting or home ownership was assumed.

Probably the most thorough study available is that provided by the U.S. Bureau of Labor in their monthly publication titled *Consumer Price Index,* which many libraries carry.

The U.S. Department of Labor's Bureau of Labor Statistics annually publishes a comparison of family budgets in urban areas. These budgets and accompanying indexes can be used to compare differ-

JOB COMPARISON FORM

Factor	Your Value	ABC CORP. Value		XYZ CORP. Value		CPA & CO. Value	
Prestige and reputation	2	2 × 5 =	10	2 × 4 =	8	2 × 2 =	4
Size of organization	0						
Growth potential (sales)	4	4 × 5 =	20	4 × 3 =	12	4 × 2 =	8
Product diversification	2	2 × 1 =	2	2 × 5 =	10	2 × 1 =	2
Management caliber	5	5 × 4 =	20	5 × 3 =	15	5 × 5 =	10
Industry choice	3	3 × 5 =	15	3 × 4 =	12	3 × 5 =	15
Interesting assignments	4	4 × 3 =	12	4 × 4 =	16	4 × 5 =	20
Early responsibility	5	5 × 2 =	10	5 × 3 =	15	5 × 4 =	20
Location	0						
Job security	0						
Salary	3	3 × 2 =	6	3 × 5 =	15	3 × 3 =	9
Training program	1	1 × 4 =	4	1 × 3 =	3	1 × 1 =	1
Fringe benefits	0						
Travel responsibilities	0						
Immediate superior	5	5 × 3 =	15	5 × 3 =	15	5 × 5 =	25
People work with	4	4 × 4 =	14	4 × 4 =	16	4 × 5 =	20
Recommendations of friends	3	3 × 4 =	12	3 × 4 =	12	3 × 2 =	6
Working conditions	3	3 × 3 =	9	3 × 4 =	12	3 × 2 =	6
Interest level of firm	4	4 × 5 =	20	4 × 4 =	16	4 × 5 =	20
Advancement opportunity	5	5 × 2 =	10	5 × 5 =	10	5 × 3 =	15
Point Total			179		187		181
Relative Ranking			3		1		2

Rate each of the factors on a scale of 5 to 0 with 5 being most important and 0 of no value to you. Place your rating (5 to 0) in the "value" column. As you gather information about a particular employer, review each factor in relation to the specific employer and assign a value of 5 to 0 to the employer for each factor beside the dotted line. Next, multiply "your value" by "employer value" ratings and place the product in the column under the employer name. When complete for all factors of each employer, add the points and rank from high to low.

Figure 7-2.

ences in price levels for regional variations. The indexes are classified for three different family income levels: lower, intermediate, and higher.

Another index is published by the U.S. Chamber of Commerce based upon the earnings of a managerial or professional person earning a realistic salary. Most Chamber offices carry this survey which is available for viewing in each local office.

Figure 7-3 is a facsimile of a cost of living chart. Given wide monthly fluctuations, this chart is not designed to be current but is used for illustrative purposes only. The given index number is of no value except in relation to how it compares with other numbers.

Salary offers in different cities can be compared by dividing each salary by its respective city's cost of living index number. Caution should be used in interpreting the results because personal life-styles vary greatly and most indexes are based on an "average" family. Figure 7-4 gives some examples in comparing different salaries in different cities. After equivalent bases have been calculated, the difference in salaries between the high and low may be viewed as money in the bank.

Starting Salary Information

Most graduates would probably like to have some idea of potential salary averages for their first them on offers. This enables a quarterly report to be prepared for all colleges to use based upon a national sample of job offers. Many placement officers share this salary data with graduating students.

In addition to getting information from the graduates, over 1,600 employers keep placement officers informed of salary offers and acceptances given to their students. The employers do this by sending carbon copies of all letters (invites, offers, and acceptances) to the placement office of the school from which the student graduates.

A check with the placement officer will produce an estimate of what might be expected in salary after graduation. Based upon background, a realistic estimate is fairly easy for an expert to predict. A range rather than an average will likely be given because the mean salary can be very misleading.

Assuming that the mean and median are fairly close, it should be remembered that one-half of the graduates will be below the median. Students with grade point averages below 2.8 (A = 4.0), few campus leadership activities, no full- or part-time related work experience generally fall below the mean and towards the lower end of the range. Individuals should not be misled by averages. This may result in graduates pricing themselves out of the job market.

BUDGET INDEXES

Urban Average	100
Metropolitan Average	102
Non-Metro Average	91
Atlanta	92
Baltimore	99
Boston	118
Chicago	103
Cincinnati	96
Cleveland	102
Dallas	91
Detroit	103
Honolulu	122
Houston	92
Indianapolis	97
Kansas City	97
Los Angeles	99
Milwaukee	106
Minneapolis	103
Nashville	91
New York	114
Philadelphia	102
Pittsburgh	95
St. Louis	97
San Francisco	107
Washington	104
Frankfurt	154
Paris	175
Tokyo	160

Figure 7-3.

job out of school and where they may expect to be, salarywise, in a few years. The college placement office can provide an idea of the likely starting salary because many offices publish a weekly or monthly report on offers being made to their students. Often amounts vary considerably by curriculum. The exact offer made will depend upon prior professional experiences, major subject, degree level, grades, leadership activities, etc., and, of course, the employer's internal salary schedule for the position for which the graduate is being considered.

It is helpful to report all offers (and final placement) in confidence to the placement officer. This helps placement people keep attuned to the marketplace so they can help current and future graduates. Most placement offices cooperate with the College Placement Council, Inc., and send weekly reports to

---

INDEXING EXAMPLES

Indianapolis Equivalent of New York

$$\frac{\text{Indianapolis Index}}{\text{New York Index}} \times \text{NYC Salary}$$

$$\frac{97}{121} \times \$20,000 = \$16,033$$

An Indianapolis salary of $16,033 equals a New York salary of $20,000.

Converting to Comparable Salaries

$$\frac{\text{Salary A}}{\text{Index A}} = X_A \qquad \frac{\text{Salary C}}{\text{Index C}} = X_C$$

$$\frac{\text{Salary B}}{\text{Index B}} = X_B \qquad \frac{\text{Salary D}}{\text{Index D}} = X_D$$

All four new salaries can be compared and the difference in cost of living accounted for.

Figure 7-4.

Inform Placement Office

Always give the college placement office information on both offers and placement. The placement office needs to know the company name, position title, location, and amount of salary. This data is kept extremely confidential and some offices do not even make it part of a student's placement file.

The primary use of such data is to assist others in the career exploration part of career planning. The basic source of career information or salary (such as that presented in this book and distributed by placement offices) comes directly from past students. Without complete cooperation from each graduating student, placement offices would find it more difficult to help others in this very important aspect of career planning. Everyone wants to have salary information available to assist in career decision making. The sharing of this information with a source that can pass it along with a high level of objectivity provides a major service to others.

Important secondary reasons to share offer and placement status play an important role as well. Colleges continually face financial problems and the first items to go out of budgets seem to be student-related services. The simplest method for justification of the placement function is to show results. If an office can show a major contribution to a high percentage of graduates, it will not get the axe.

Aside from career planning, salary information aids current graduates because honest and open salary information tends to raise the overall level of salaries. The average becomes the base which many employers use in determining an appropriate salary offer. Open salary data tends to narrow the range of offers by eliminating the "lowball" offers because employers do not want to risk a potential for a negative reputation. Employers are less likely to make noncompetitive offers if they know students have a high knowledge level of their job worth.

Placement offices use placement statistics to recruit employers. Success brings further success. Employers listen to each other and recruit at colleges where qualified candidates have been found in the past.

Placement officers quickly learn who the cooperating students are and make special efforts to help that group of students. A referral by a well-respected placement officer to a key employer or job is almost a guarantee for an interview. This referral assistance may not be needed while in college, but most placement offices also assist alumni job research efforts. The employer's door is not as open to a job changer with experience as it is to the current graduating students. A little help from a friendly placement officer often provides the needed door opener.

PLACEMENT RECORD

NAME _____

EMPLOYER _____

POSITION _____

SALARY $ _____ PER MONTH

NEW ADDRESS _____

_____

Figure 7-5.

```
┌─────────────────────────────────────┐
│                                     │
│            OFFER REPORT             │
│                                     │
│   NAME _____│
│                                     │
│   EMPLOYER _____│
│                                     │
│   POSITION _____│
│                                     │
│   SALARY $_____ PER MONTH    │
│   (base amount only)                │
│                                     │
└─────────────────────────────────────┘
```

Figure 7-6.

Lastly, the federal government requires colleges to make a reasonable effort to contact all graduates and report placement status. The government is very involved in providing financial aid for students. The government wants new students coming into an institution to be aware of the marketability of the training they will be obtaining from the institution. If an incoming student requests information about the placement status of past graduates of a given curriculum, it is the institution's responsibility to provide it. Obviously, the information must come from graduating students. There is some concern that someday a degree will not be awarded until graduates have reported whether or not they have a job.

In summary, each student must decide whether or not to cooperate and give salary and placement information to the college placement office. Some people have convictions regarding secrecy. Other people believe in more openness. With the high level of confidentiality guaranteed, it makes good sense to cooperate.

Desired Salary

Most employers will ask on their company job applications what is expected for a desired salary. Employers have relatively narrow salary ranges for each type of job for which they normally consider college graduates. An individual's niche in the range will depend on the factors mentioned earlier and, perhaps most importantly, the current supply and demand for people interested in that field.

There are a number of ways to approach the problem of what desired salary to request. Asking for too much will eliminate some offers because the candidate knows a rejection will be forthcoming. When asking for too little, there is the possibility that that is all the employer will offer. There is less danger of the latter because employers assume others might be in-terested in the same individual, and the employer does not want to risk losing a good candidate based on a low salary figure.

One sound suggestion is to suggest to the employer a salary range. This lets the employer know the candidate is not overly concerned about an exact amount and that an estimate of one's own potential is known. This method usually finds an overlap between the candidate's perceived range and the employer's given range for the job. Of course, candidates can verbally defend why their offers should be near the top of the range by documenting above-average qualifications.

Another idea is to give the mean offer being extended to others with the same major and degree level. This gives the employer an idea of expectations and shows reasonable judgment. The figure can be verbally defended at the appropriate final interview, if asked, and additional support can be produced based upon credentials.

It is not out of line to simply leave the salary line on the application blank. There is no stigma attached to this idea. Most employers have a firm notion of what they will offer regardless of what is proposed.

One last suggestion is that if a minimum salary figure is firmly in mind below which the job will not be accepted, the candidate should let the employer know this. If, because of certain reasons, such as having other job offers, being on a leave of absence from another position, possessing extensive related experience, etc., offers below a certain amount are unacceptable, it is best to be honest with the employer and state this also. There is no advantage to wasting the time of both parties if an agreement cannot be reached. Many MBA graduates with prior experience use this method to help screen potential employers. Employers will appreciate these candid views.

Salary is seldom the overriding reason for accepting or declining an offer. It is best to let the employer know that salary is an important variable, if it is, but also that it is only one of the criteria that will be used in a final analysis of which position to accept. There are other variables which may be more important than salary.

Many college graduates can make more money by tending bar or becoming cocktail waitresses, but few of them eventually elect those career paths. Prime factors in the decision will center on the type of work, its interesting and challenging nature, and the possible potential for further advancement and growth. Values and maturity level come through loud if stress is put on dollars.

Negotiating Salary

A starting salary is not a topic for negotiation with most potential employers. If it is discussed at all, it will be discussed at the time of the secondary interviews. If asked, it is best to give an idea of expectations. The prospective employer needs a straight answer. With this statement and a candidate's credentials the employer decides on a firm salary that is consistent with the company's internal salary schedule. Once the figure is offered, it is not likely to change.

If an attempt to renegotiate the salary amount is made by the candidate, the offer may be lost. An offer can be withdrawn at any time prior to acceptance in addition to simply terminating it with the date the employer gives for the response. If it is certain that the offer is unacceptable, nothing is lost by asking the employer to reconsider. Although the offer probably will be withdrawn, there is always the possibility that if the employer really needs an individual's talents, the offer may be increased.

Frankly, it is not worth the risk. If money must be coaxed from the employer, a bad start is made. The employer may not be happy later because of the issue or may take it from the first raise anyway. All good employers reward productivity. Showing what can be achieved by work will produce later rewards. It is dangerous to get caught asking someone to provide rewards based only on potential.

Future Salary

Very little information is available about what to expect after several years into a career path. When questioned about future salary potentials, few employers volunteer what the future may hold because few of them can or are willing to predict the future. Potential earnings depend on ability and motivation—also being at the right place at the right time.

But rather than blind luck, the "movers" in any organization tend to make their own "breaks" happen. The pyramid gets narrower and narrower as one moves toward the top.

An excellent source of salary information is in the form of the U.S. Government Salary Schedule. The grades and various levels within the grades are closely attached to given job titles for government jobs. Exact salaries are given for each salary grade and years of experience at that level. These salaries are determined by Congress after extensive salary surveys of equivalent jobs in business and industry. There is a conscious effort by government representatives to keep the schedule competitive, yet not far above comparable jobs in industry, so the government has a fair chance of attracting equally talented individuals. Libraries, placement offices, and most government offices have the salary schedules available for perusal.

Figure 7-7 gives annual salaries for a selected number of positions within government and comparable jobs in industry. It is necessary to add about 5% for each year since October, 1976, to get an approximate figure for today. The point is not to identify positions or salary potential from Figure 7-7 but to get a feel for how to go about making a realistic estimate of potential.

Another excellent source of salary information in selected career fields is classified advertisements. Many give a salary range for a given number of years of experience for the position available. The interested party must temper the ad, however, with some judgment because many of these ads are "come-ons" designed to elicit a massive amount of resumes from potential candidates. Nonetheless, many of the jobs are filled at the salary ranges quoted so they do offer a clue toward future earnings.

The most extensive listings of want ads are in the

SALARY COMPARISON GOVERNMENT AND INDUSTRY

	Government	Industry
Chief accountant	30,500	33,900
Experienced accountant	21,800	23,400
Experienced auditor	18,300	20,000
Accountant	15,000	15,400
Mid-level job analyst	12,400	13,600
Engineer (near top)	35,600	43,700
Engineering technician	15,000	16,000
Beginning engineer	10,100	13,900
Personnel director (experienced)	26,000	26,800
Buyer	18,300	20,000

Note: Government pay is "fourth step" rate for workers with several years of experience in the job. Private pay is from U.S. Bureau of Labor Statistics Survey of October 1976. More current data must be approximate for industry and government can be obtained from a general schedule.

Figure 7-7.

daily newspapers of the major metropolitan areas. Large libraries carry newspapers from many cities so it is possible to review several papers, and not just a local paper. Sunday editions usually contain the most help wanted positions.

Also, information can be obtained from want ads that are placed by employers in their major trade publications. Most of the industries (automotive, chemical, petroleum, retailing, insurance, etc.) and selected fields (data processing, accounting, sales, production, etc.) have related monthly or quarterly periodicals that offer a classified ad service to members. For example, *Automotive News* and the *Wall Street Journal* have sections where employers may place advertisements for talent. Most of the positions available will require experience, so new graduates can see where they might be on the salary scale with a given level of years of experience.

From time to time, surveys of executive compensation are made by management consultants, university professors, and business research institutes. Major business libraries at universities carry these. Some of the major business periodicals (*Business Week, Commerce, Nation's Business,* etc.) summarize these in their regular issues.

In 1973, this author completed an extensive study on career performance of 1,100 Master of Business Administration graduates of 1962 from 16 major business schools with national reputations. Over 80% were employed in business and held upper middle management positions. Over 70% were still em-

ployed with their first or second employer since graduating which indicates that the "movers" were not the job-hoppers. The 85% employed in a salary position had quadrupled their starting salary and had a net worth of over $100,000. The 15% employed in their own business earned slightly more. Over one-half of them work more than 50 hours per week. Over 70% considered themselves as functioning in finance, marketing, or general management positions in contrast to specialized functions such as engineering, data processing, legal, etc. The average age was 37 years with most of the MBA's working in large firms. Studies similar to this are published occasionally and give an important insight into career potential.

Needless to say, everyone beginning a career does not move into middle or top management. Few make it or even care to move that far. There are many graduates who would prefer a comfortable salary (not $30,000 plus), an interesting line of work (not a pressure-packed daily challenge), a 40-50 hour work week (not the 50-80 hour week of top managers), and a high degree of involvement in community and family life (not company life). As discussed in Chapter 1, compromises have to be made along the way. Since career planning is an on-going process, values are likely to change as one gets older, and consequently, trade-offs regarding the preferred lifestyle will be made.

Throughout the past decade salary increases to the new college hire often progressed at a faster clip

PROJECTED ANNUAL SALARY

Starting Salary	Years Since Graduation									
	1	2	3	4	5	6	7	8	9	10
$10,000	$10,700	$11,450	$12,250	$13,000	$13,750	$14,600	$15,300	$16,050	$16,900	$17,750
12,000	12,850	13,750	14,700	15,600	16,500	17,500	18,400	19,300	20,250	21,300
14,000	15,000	16,000	17,150	18,200	19,300	20,400	21,450	22,500	23,650	24,800
16,000	17,100	18,300	19,600	20,800	22,000	23,350	24,500	25,750	27,000	28,400
18,000	19,250	20,600	22,050	23,350	24,800	26,250	27,600	29,000	30,400	31,900
20,000	21,400	22,900	24,500	26,000	27,500	29,200	30,600	32,100	33,800	35,500
Increases	Assumes 7% increase			Assumes 6% increase			Assumes 5% increase			

A more realistic example might assume a $1,000 promotion at the end of three years and a $1,500 promotion at the end of six years.

Figure 7-8.

than salary increases to present employees. Many experts believe, due to the changing supply-demand situation between college graduates and entry-level jobs, that the next decade will bring salary increases at a faster pace to junior, middle, and top management personnel.

The "compression effect" was a great problem for the current employees' counterparts of a few years ago. Rapidly rising entry-level salaries kept pushing middle range salary positions into an even slower rising upper salary range position. In other words, the spread between the entry-level salary and top compensation in the salary grades kept getting narrower.

This contributed to dissatisfaction and high turnover among bright young people. In selected companies and industries, this could still be a problem. If individuals get caught in the middle, they may be forced to make some tough personal decisions. Graduates should be prepared for it.

CONTINUATION OF CAREER PLANNING

Once having evaluated several employers and accepted a position, the job campaign must stop. A person can take no more interviews or evaluate subsequent job offers even if the contact came before the acceptance. The first acceptance is binding! The point of no return has been passed. The newly hired employee is not alone in making an unequivocal decision; the future employer notifies other candidates that the position has been filled. The employer may talk with a better qualified applicant later but a bind-

ing commitment has been made. Both parties have made a promise and given their word. Only extreme hardship or grave consequences should be permitted to influence either party's position on this matter.

The career planning, however, does not end. Energies should be concentrated on learning more about the new position and begin preparing for it. The first job after college can influence a career thrust more than the actual academic preparation for it. Potential failure is a difficult prospect to face particularly if there are no alternatives on how to get around it. This is not to say that if problems develop they cannot be met, but it is best to mobilize forces to insure that the decision made is a wise one. If the new employee is prepared, the decision will be a wise one.

Turnover

Interruption of a career path is a high price to pay. Re-starting the career planning process, especially the placement function, often delays career advancement. Once employed, the placement process reaches high expenditure levels. Expenses include resume reproduction, postage, agencies fees, moving expenses, etc.

A psychological cost is inherent in job changes. There is always the pressing question about whether the change is wise and a burden to bear if the reason for the change is failure on the initial job. An early job change is something to be avoided if at all possible. This fact highlights the necessity for thoroughly analyzing the reasons for selection of the initial employer after college.

The cost of a lost employee is great for

employers as well. Given the time and expense involved in recruiting, advertising, staff time, relocating, etc., employers lose a large initial investment if the new employee leaves early. In addition to salary, most employers have a major investment in benefits, facilities, staff time, and training for each employee. Losing an employee is money down the drain.

Clearly it behooves employer and employee to keep turnover at the lowest possible point. However, unforseen circumstances sometimes occur that force employers to terminate employees for lack of business or poor performance. Circumstances occur that demand that the employee seek other employment because of a better opportunity or to avoid being terminated.

Turnover among college graduates is not as great as newspaper stories sometimes indicate. A recent survey showed that 26% of new employees had left employers during the first three years. Figure 7-9 gives some more specific information. Turnover normally drops markedly after the first three years as employees adjust to the organization and see a specific career path ahead. With most organizations, turnover among college level employees is extremely low after an employee has accumulated over five years of experience with the organization.

As a rule, job changers move from large to small organizations. Larger organizations tend to promote from within and small firms often prefer to buy talent rather than grow talent. Larger firms tend to pay higher salaries but promote people at a slower pace. Most top officers, whether large or small firms, have been with the organization in middle management for several years. The average age of chief officers is over 55 years so do not be mislead by the news stories that discuss the exceptional person who makes top management before age 45.

A high percentage of college level employees who leave their initial employer within the first three years return to graduate school. Some individuals discover a lack of skills to handle job pressure and return to school to develop new tools or refresh old skills. Unfortunately for some, returning to college is an easier way to avoid admitting failure in the world of work than solving the real problem.

Returning to graduate school may be a necessity for future advancement. The return should be part of a broader career plan. It appears that the need for refresher and continuing education is a growing trend among managerial, technical, and professional personnel. Many employers support the concept although very few will pay for further education unless it is done on a part-time basis.

The Transition

The change from a college campus to an employing organization may be an abrupt one. The vocational theorists discussed in Chapter 1 view this as a transition stage in which a test of preparation for reality is being conducted. The success of reality testing depends to a large extent upon career planning. If a valid impression of self-concept has been developed and the potential world of work for people with like qualifications has been thoroughly explored, the reality test should present no difficulty.

The abruptness hits when graduates suddenly find themselves not being treated as part of an elite group of college students. Like freshmen in college they must start over again to prove themselves to new colleagues who may be somewhat reluctant to accommodate them and their ideas. People are likely to be the greatest challenge, not the job content!

Adjustment

Popular magazines and newspapers frequently write stories about the difficult adjustment that col-

TURNOVER RATES OF COLLEGE GRADUATES

	First Year	Second Year	Third Year	Three Year Total
Men: Engineering and technical	8%	8%	7%	23%
Men: Business and non-technical	11	12	10	33
Women: All Fields	14	12	10	36

Based on 1975 Endicott Report of 160 employers. A later survey in 1977 showed a median of 26 percent of turnover after three years. Turnover continues to be less in technical than non-technical fields.

Figure 7-9.

lege graduates make when entering the work force. The adjustment is a maturing process. Moving smoothly from one social situation to a strange situation requires attention to details that may never have been important in the past. A smooth transition demands that new employees anticipate the future. Problems develop because the attitudes of other employees are not always positively disposed toward college graduates.

A recent report cited in Figure 7-10 highlights the adjustment problems college graduates often face. Employers anticipate problems and make appropriate allowances. Actually, wise graduates eliminate any adjustment problems by planning ahead.

One can readily analyze the list of potential adjustment problems and develop a constructive approach to deal with each problem. The difficulty in laying out a plan when there is little comprehension of the new work setting results from uncertainty. Because of these problems, many employers lean toward hiring prior co-op or professional internship students to minimize the transitional problems.

Cooperative education and other types of experiential learning programs appear to be the future trend. More universities and employers are working together to foster this mutual teaching and learning program. Any student having an option to participate in such a program should immediately exercise the option. To expedite the adjustment process, and enhance interviewing success, the internship is well worth the added cost in time needed to complete a given degree.

Often college graduates take unrealistic salary expectations to the organization. The United States is basically a middle class society where only a very small percentage of the population earn over $25,000. For some reason many expect that such a high salary is characteristic of most college graduates when in fact less than 10% of the population earns over $25,000. Less than 20% of college graduates earned over $25,000 in 1976.

Figure 7-11 gives the median income in the United States at $10,755 which is about the income at which most college graduates start. Upward salary progression is not as rapid as most people anticipate. The median salaries quoted for jobs in various job categories include only those select groups of high achievers who made it to a high level in an organization.

BEGINNING A CAREER

When reporting to work everyone around may be busy with their responsibilities and have little time to share. The new employee's attitude must remain friendly, courteous, and eager to learn and accept direct assignments. It is advantageous to learn the names, job functions, and personalities of all people contacted in performing assignments as soon as possible. Secretaries and part-time people should not be overlooked—everyone is important!

The first few assignments are unlikely to tax prior training or professional abilities. Employers will think that they are quickly offering responsibility, and new employees are likely to think otherwise. Respect for a new employee's abilities will come with time. It is imperative that the new employee refrain from criticizing others. It is equally important to

---

ADJUSTMENT PROBLEMS OF COLLEGE GRADUATES

1. Relating theory to practice: the transition
2. Adjusting to work routines: hours and scheduling
3. Adjusting to corporate struction: business operations
4. Unrealistic expectations: too much too soon
5. Developing cooperative attitudes: people differences
6. Accepting responsibility, decision making: completing jobs
7. Understanding management philosophy: profit motive
8. Recognizing inadequacies: finding themselves
9. Adjusting to new location: different lifestyles
10. Learning to communicate effectively: writing

Source: Endicott Report, 1977. Responses in order from 165 companies asked to indicate the most difficult problems which new graduates face in adjusting to employment in business.

Figure 7-10.

EDUCATION AND INCOME

High School Graduate	$10,910
1-3 Years of College	12,541
4 Plus Years of College	15,419
Median Income	10,755

Source: U.S. Bureau of the Census, 1976. Median based on white males.

Figure 7-11.

learn internal practices and politics quickly. Even if employers do not have a formal training program, they will be trying to accomplish the same goals as any program designed to aid new people:

1. To integrate people and their ideas into the organization as rapidly as possible.
2. To provide them with background information on the organization, its people, and its products.
3. To nurture an environment conducive to immediate productivity.

The three most common methods of training college graduates are rotational work assignments, formal classroom instruction, and on-the-job training. It is likely all methods will be experienced at different points during the first year.

There will be a considerable amount of training by observing others, and a quick understanding of various aspects of the job is expected. This will enable the new employee to learn as much as possible about the jobs of other people. Even while never being expected to perform these jobs, exposure to other people is being achieved. It may be necessary for the new employee to call on other individuals for help in completing a project so an understanding of the jobs others do is important.

A balance between critical thinking and sensitivity to the feelings of others must be developed. New employees should present their ideas by tactfully asking the right questions, while at the same time being prepared for criticism. Mistakes will be made, and embarrassing situations caused by another person may occur in front of a superior. If mistakes are not made, it is likely that not enough is being done. The first few months mistakes will be discounted.

Above all, it should be remembered that others are proud of their organization and what they contribute. The same high level of organization enthusiasm is expected from everyone.

APPRAISING PERFORMANCE

Many graduates get extremely frustrated during the first year. Based on all the long hours and hard work, they may be surprised to learn that the salary increases the first year do not measure up to expectations. Few employers offer more than a 5% to 7% annual raise during the first two or three years on the job. Financial rewards are not likely to start materializing until after the third year when a solid track record has been made.

Most employers conduct an oral performance appraisal every six to twelve months. The parties concerned will sit down and review accomplishments of the past period. This may mean a harsh critique *just* as if a professor was giving a final course grade.

Some graduates find this process hard to accept because they have never been criticized to their faces. They become defensive. The outcome of a personal review is not to defend the past but to plan the future. Most superiors will set concrete, obtainable, yet high, objective standards to be met. Participation is required! It should be assumed that responsibilities are attainable. Accountability will be demanded.

During a person's twenties, most employers expect a very high level of productivity. After the first year of learning and making mistakes, people are expected to perform competently in their field. Work will now be done at a professional level. Every project and assignment will be thoroughly analyzed to evaluate abilities, interests, and motivation.

Because of the long time frame, some graduates do not realize that they are being evaluated and get bored and dissatisfied. They do not feel management is observing their performance. Even if the career goal is to open a business of one's own, before the age of 30, it is necessary to do one's best to get a variety of work assignments with one employer.

Surveys of top executives invariably suggest that those who "make it" show great loyalty to their employers and have been employed with them for many years. Job hoppers seldom move into major responsibilities. Several recent studies of MBA graduates who were now in management positions divide their samples into a job hopper group and stable group. The studies indicate that the job hoppers do make short-run gains at the expense of their long-term ambitions. For MBA graduates who have been out of school for ten years, the job hopper group perceive that they hold higher position levels in the organization, but the stable group commands higher earnings. Thus, it is best for graduates to plan to weather some difficult times with an employer.

CAREER PROGRESS

During the age span of the twenties, employees may begin to receive promotions to junior supervisory positions. During this time management will be watching their abilities to deal with people problems. First promotions to important supervisory positions occur around the age of 30. They may be responsible for the work of a few professional employees and several clerical and production individuals. They may be asked to assume responsibility for a high level of sales volume, budget, expense accounts, and/or physical facilities.

The manner in which responsibility is accepted and work assignments through others are accomplished will have a lasting effect on long-range career plans. Knowledge of psychology and management principles, coupled with common sense, should demonstrate the talent for planning, motivating people, and obtaining results.

As a career progresses, career planning should continue to concentrate on developing innate ability and improving education. Taking inventory (self-assessment) every year or two will help keep a career perspective in mind while crystallizing a personal philosophy.

Career progress can be enhanced by following a number of practices that others have used in moving up in their organizations. Figure 7-12 offers some ideas which may be useful. Some of these ideas conflict or are not applicable to every individual. A personal scheme should be developed and written out so that an occasional review will indicate how closely the plan is being followed. Many people know what to do to aid success, but just do not follow their plans.

THE NEXT JOB CHANGE

All of the admonishment to stick with an employer during times when little progress in the career plan is seen should not be taken to mean that one may never want to make a job change. If a dead end is perceived, the necessity for a job change must be faced. However, many experts see a softening in the job market at the professional level. More individuals are likely to remain with their present employers. Even at management levels, seniority, in addition to productivity, plays an important role in who is going to be asked to leave for budgetary reasons.

In the long run, the only security is ability and productivity. When abilities are unrecognized, the dissatisfied employee should accept the challenge and start organizing a new job campaign. The methods of accomplishing this are much similar to those suggested in earlier chapters.

FORTY ACTION IDEAS FOR ADVANCEMENT

Seek additional responsibilities.
Complete assignments immediately.
Make suggestions instead of critical reviews.
Solve problems instead of just identifying.
Praise others for good work.

Develop new skills through training.
Seek assignments that offer exposure to managers.
Search for the reason behind each assignment.
Look at problems from a management viewpoint.
Do not underestimate your social responsibilities.

Nurture personal friendships in your peer group.
Ask for certain work assignments.
Study the normal promotional channels.
Develop your personal life outside the organization.
Make professional contacts outside the organization.

Seek line, not staff, responsibilities.
Be patient for rewards but go after challenges.
Beware of "assistant to" titles. Watch go-fers.
Avoid internal politics and cliques.
Show your enthusiasm for the organization.

Discuss ideas, never people.
Advertise your abilities by superior performances.
Keep records of your work to show later.
Work on your public speaking skills.
Talk to subordinates as friends. They make you.

Never allow pressures to compromise quality.
Maintain personal and organizational ethics.
Make a written appraisal each year for your review.
Ask your superiors for advice about your career.
No negative criticism does not equal positive praise.

Rate your supervisors' promotional possibilities.
Get help if an assignment is over your head.
Accept criticism and ask for it. Use it to improve.
Never argue.
Rethink your plans if the pressure bothers you.
Be prepared to relocate if promotion merits it.

Maintain organizational loyalty and advertise it.
Learn to delegate authority.
Accept blame for poor work of subordinates.
Expect two to three year plateaus in promotion.
Watch for earning ceilings.

Figure 7-12.

Before deciding to make a job change, the employee should go through the same type of self-assessment discussed earlier. The discovery may be made that the problem is not in the organization.

```
HUMAN RELATIONS IN ACTION

"I admit that I made a mistake"
"You did an excellent job"
"What is your opinion"
"If you please"
"Thank you"
"We"
"I"
```

Figure 7-13.

Perhaps some corrective personal action is necessary when making the move.

It will help to analyze on paper why it has become necessary to leave the present employer. A list of all of the advantages of staying with the present employer should be made. Even though a new employer may pay more and offer a promotion, it will take time to achieve acceptance.

New employers recognize that a high percentage of job candidates on the job market just could not make it with their present employer. Their hiring standards are, therefore, much higher than those for the first job after college. Even if employees do not get fired, many leave because they are subtly told to "look around" or they anticipate the situation before it develops. One should be prepared to have future employers ask why the change is desired. Many may not accept the true answer given.

Before a decision to leave has been made, it might be wise for the employee to request a transfer to a different department. There are great benefits in remaining with the present employer.

Many experts suggest that a change is not worth the cost and related risk unless earnings can be increased by at least 20%. Of course, this would be higher if a move involving a household was necessary.

An employed person should always remember, "Never quit the present job until a new job offer is obtained." It is much more difficult to look around while unemployed for two major reasons. First, funds are usually limited because no income is being generated, and few people can afford to survive long without an income. Secondly, many employers will hesitate hiring someone who is unemployed.

Looking around while employed presents some difficult problems also. Getting time off to interview with a prospective employer usually means taking a vacation day and too many of those can alert the present employer. Most employers will terminate employment immediately if they know a person is

```
REASONS GRADUATES CHANGE JOBS

1. Lack of advancement—progress too slow
2. Higher salary
3. Preferred another location
4. Terminated—poor performance
5. Disinterest in work performed
6. Returning to graduate school
7. Changed career goals—lacked goals
8. Disliked travel and working hours
9. Reduction in force by firm—cut-backs

Source: Endicott Study, 1977. Responses in order by
148 firms asked to list the reasons why graduates
changed jobs.
```

Figure 7-14.

looking around. Since it is necessary to put out "feelers," there is always the chance that word will get back to the present employer by an unrecognized grapevine.

Unlike campus interviewing, it is usually not possible to interview with several employers, wait for their offers, and then objectively decide which one is the best. Once the offer is tendered, a specific, but limited, time in which to make a decision is established. If a person can look ahead before accepting the first job after college and see the multitude of problems in making a change later, hopefully it will motivate investigation and planning for that first job.

The first job after college provides the thrust behind all future career direction and is the best reason for planning well.

A job change is occasionally a necessary element in a sound career plan. However, it is not normally a pleasant situation for the person changing jobs or the person's family and close friends. Roots must be pulled up. Although it is not healthy to make a habit of changing jobs, it is necessary to be prepared to make a shift if the situation demands it. It is not something of which to be ashamed. The mechanics of making the change are nearly identical to those suggested in earlier chapters. Even if earnings are above $20,000 and the services of a search firm are used, it will be necessary to follow the same procedures recommended earlier in this book.

CONTINUING EDUCATION

Since consideration of a career is now under way, thought about working for an advanced degree to better prepare for the career may have also developed. Unfortunately, there is no clear-cut answer to the question, "Should I go on to graduate school?" To be sure, it is best to consider *all* alternatives and graduate study is a major alternative.

There is a strong view in the United States that the more education held, the greater the chances for success. This is not always true. A person can be overtrained and underemployed. It may be true that further education is not going to hurt, but it may not help either.

The answer to the graduate school question largely depends on the *type of position* eventually desired. Thousands of high school graduates earn substantially more than Ph.D. recipients; so if a person is measuring success in strictly monetary terms, it may be hard to make a strong case in favor of graduate school.

Is It Necessary?

The starting point for arriving at this decision is to first look at the position desired. Can the position be obtained without the advanced degree? In many positions, a person can advance just as far without the graduate degree. For many students, the investment demands at least an annual $15,000 commitment in out-of-pocket cost and lost income each year.

The position aspired to may well be worth it if the degree is required. On the other hand, if the position can be obtained now and the degree can be completed part-time or with a leave of absence later, that may be the wiser path to follow.

In 1977, Dr. Frank Endicott asked the 215 employers in his annual survey if their firm had a tuition reimbursement plan for employees with the bachelor degree if the employee wished to take graduate courses. Over 90% indicated that they did have such a plan but 93% required that the courses be job related.

The Variables

There are so many variables to the graduate school question that no one can provide the answer without hedging. The academic community stresses advanced degrees for qualified students while the employment market hedges or says "no." It is a difficult choice. The individual must investigate the pros and cons, financial commitments, etc., in conjunction with immediate and long-range career goals. This will create a better position from which to make a decision.

Which graduate degree to pursue depends on long-term career interests. People in liberal arts who wish to continue in their undergraduate field must question the value of additional education unless they wish to teach in the area. One should keep in mind that the openings for master degreed people are limited.

For those who wish to teach in higher education or become a professional in their field (sociologist, psychologist, historian, writer, etc.), they may need the doctorate degree. Most schools encourage work toward the doctorate immediately after obtaining the undergraduate degree because time can be conserved. Few business firms pay more for a master's degree in a liberal arts field.

For a business undergraduate, the value of additional training has to be questioned. Is this going to mean more of the same? To avoid this, one would surely want to earn an advanced degree from another institution. Most business undergraduates already have over two years of business courses which is equivalent to the two years in many MBA degree programs that an engineer, liberal arts, or science graduate will have upon graduation.

A person may wish to change career direction by choosing a professional or technical advanced degree. The two most popular currently are the MBA and the JD degrees. These will be discussed in some depth later in this chapter. There are other options. Some of them are in the fields of public service, social service, paramedical, allied health, mass communications, journalism, medical school, etc. However, a person should keep some perspective on how abilities and interests relate to the career field for which these programs prepare a person.

Sometimes more education can restrict employment possibilities. Nearly everyone knows another person who has been rejected for a job opening because of being "overqualified." The individual could have handled the assignment but often is not given the chance. Why? One reason is that the individual's expectations and hence job satisfaction are inconsistent with the assignment. They would get bored and be unproductive. Another reason is that the employer figures that the job would simply be a temporary assignment until a position more in line with their education is found. Considering the high cost of training before becoming productive and the high cost of turnover, why take the risk, especially when other qualified applicants are available? It is best to avoid this unpleasant box.

Last Alternative

Some graduates approach graduate study as a last alternative. "If I cannot find suitable employment, I can always go on to graduate study." That attitude is likely to cause great disillusionment and

unrewarding career performance. Jobs are most plentiful for undergraduates with wide ranges of career alternatives that they can pursue.

As the education level increases, specialty increases and the range of alternatives narrows. The number of jobs within the specialty must by definition decrease. What employer would hire a master or doctorate graduate to do a job that an undergraduate can be hired to do? Why risk the dissatisfaction? Why overpay for the job? This line of reasoning, whether the potential graduate student is in agreement or not with its conclusion, deserves consideration.

The fact is that some undergraduates decide on graduate study because they could not get a job—or did not even try hard—after college. The reason for their lack of success may relate to their lack of a positive undergraduate record, personality, or lack of clear career goals. Graduate study can make that person even more unemployable.

One of the most difficult MBA graduates to place is the person who did not rank high in the MBA class and also did not make an outstanding undergraduate record—a mediocre record all the way around; an average undergraduate record and an average MBA record. There is some validity to the argument that if a person cannot get at least three offers as an undergraduate, *one* would not be received with an advanced degree. Employers simply raise their standards for advanced degree candidates, not just the requirement of the degree.

Few people are expert judges of their own abilities. A possible solution here is to let employers judge capabilities as an undergraduate when the standards are much lower. For the person having difficulty, graduate study is not the likely solution to improving marketability except under the circumstance where the degree is a requirement for the job desired.

A very valid reason for returning to graduate study is to change a career thrust. Engineers, teachers, accountants, sales people, etc., all may return to beef-up skills in their area or to switch into such fields as finance, law, public service, etc.

The old adage that once leaving campus, the student will never return is false! Training in a highly technical society cannot stop with either a bachelor or master degree. As continuing education programs in universities continue to grow professionally, so will individuals.

Whether the individual decides to continue an education now, later, or part-time is not nearly as important as what direction that career should take. Once a particular area of graduate study is decided upon, to a large extent, the individual is locked into a career path.

By beginning work in education, business, or public service immediately after graduation with a bachelor degree, those unhappy with their career direction can always quit and return to school. All types of potential employers who seek the advanced degree will feel that returning for graduate study was an acceptable reason for leaving the last employer.

GRADUATE SCHOOL COSTS

Since costs vary considerably between universities, a universal analytical cost cannot be calculated. But given a specific university, it should be possible to approximate the costs by using the model in Figure 7-15.

It is almost impossible to analytically calculate at what point an investment in graduate school is recovered. Typically, the person with the higher degree will start at a higher rate, but the individual who started two years before should be earning more than this higher starting rate. It is difficult for an em-

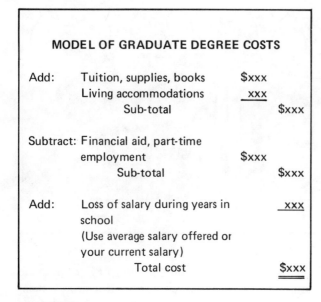

MODEL OF GRADUATE DEGREE COSTS

Add:	Tuition, supplies, books	$xxx
	Living accommodations	xxx
	Sub-total	$xxx
Subtract:	Financial aid, part-time employment	$xxx
	Sub-total	$xxx
Add:	Loss of salary during years in school	xxx
	(Use average salary offered or your current salary)	
	Total cost	$xxx

Figure 7-15.

ployer to justify paying a beginner, regardless of degrees, more money than the individual with two years of experience.

Assuming that the master degreed person shortly catches up with the experienced candidate, salary progress of both will largely depend on individual abilities. Those persons with advanced degrees and superior knowledge are right to assume that they would advance faster. If they do not, they cannot recover their investment. If they do, the differential between annual salaries is the increment that begins paying off the principle of the original investment.

In other words, it is best to base the decision about graduate study on factors other than financial return. Other than an intuitive guess, no one can provide a concrete answer. It is a personal decision.

Most employers will pick up all, or at least part, of the education bill if the employee is attending a university part-time program while employed full time. Only a few employers have scholarship programs where they send outstanding employees back to graduate school on a full-time basis, grant them leave of absence, and pay some portion of their expenses. Normally, to be eligible, they must be employed full time with the firm for a certain number of years.

Generally speaking, a firm will not pay the complete bill for this education. Before paying any portion, with most firms the individual must be employed for at least an initial period before becoming eligible for these special benefits. In most cases, the field of study must have some relationship to the present position or the one the employee is seeking.

Many employers will grant a leave of absence to attend graduate school. This is an implied guarantee that the same or better position will be waiting after completing the degree. In many cases, benefits, insurance, and vacation and seniority continue to accrue while on leave. This is a substantial commitment by many employers who have very liberal benefit plans.

GETTING ADMITTED

Assuming graduate study is affordable, the next step is to determine whether or not one can gain admission. Each university and degree program establish their own requirements for admission. There are common elements that all schools and departments share in making the evaluative decision on whether or not to admit students. These elements are used as predictors of one's ability to succeed in the degree program.

Testing

Nearly all degree programs require that a battery of tests be taken to determine an individual's ability to succeed in the program. These tests contain both verbal and qualitative sections and the schools place varying degrees of emphasis on the sections, depending upon their academic orientation. The most common of the national standardized tests are the Graduate Record Examination (GRE), the Law School Admissions Test (LSAT), and the Graduate Management Admission Test (GMAT). Any university can provide details on these tests. They require no preparation.

G.P.A.

Grade point average is almost always used as a guide to determine academic abilities. It is really the only measure of past performance available. Most schools require at least a B + average.

Transcripts

Applicants are required to send a copy of their transcript from each school attended. The transcripts will be analyzed for specific courses taken, grades in these courses, and any positive or negative grade trends by year in college.

Faculty References

Most schools require at least two letters from previous instructors recommending the applicant for admission. It is always important for students to get to know as many professors as possible, particularly during the junior and senior years in college so that they can remember individuals and provide favorable recommendations.

Other Factors

If the applicant does not "make the grade" on one of the points above, occasionally some school will make an exception or admit the person on probation. Some favorable points in the factors listed below might give them a reason for considering the applicant as an exception:

Work experience
Military experience
Grade point average the last two years
Grades in the major subject particularly if it relates to the proposed field of study
Maturity
Personal interviews
Goals and objective in obtaining the degree

THE MBA DEGREE

Since the Master of Business Administration degree is so popular among liberal arts, sciences, engineers, and business undergraduates, some details about this degree and law school are discussed. Before considering either degree, the decision should be made as to what is wanted. The MBA degree is oriented toward business although government officials, educational administrators, small businessmen, and others may find the degree helpful.

The applicant should decide where interest exists, whether in accounting, finance, marketing, production, industrial relations, etc., before selecting a school. Different schools have different reputations and certain employers may not send recruiters to the school chosen if the program in a given subject area is not highly respected. Potential graduate students should do some investigating of schools, and recognize that there are advantages and disadvantages to obtaining the degree.

MBA Degree Advantages

Although there are few well-defined employer policies regarding the MBA degree, receipt of the degree offers several distinct advantages over applicants that do not possess it. In fact, some companies, although only a few, recruit only MBA's for a limited number of openings in special programs specifically designed for MBA graduates. In most companies the MBA's will start in the same positions as undergraduates but because of their advanced training, MBA's should advance at a more rapid pace. The MBA degree usually insures a higher starting salary—about $2,000 more per year.

The MBA gives most candidates a competitive edge. With the additional training, they should perform better on the job and because of the initial salary received, the employer will probably want to advance them more rapidly in the organization. The degree should also enhance chances for promotions when being compared to candidates whose job performance is similar but without the MBA degree.

The level of maturity should be more beneficial to an employer after two more years of study. Many changes take place between the ages of 22 to 24 years. In fact, one of the reasons suggested for the higher salaries at some of the better known MBA programs is that the average age of the graduating classes has been over 26 years. This implies that many graduates either have prior work experience or meaningful military service for which employers pay a premium.

Hopefully in any MBA program there will be taught many more sophisticated business tools and techniques not normally covered in undergraduate business schools. Also, the quality of instruction and depth of study will be found to be much higher than in undergraduate programs.

MBA Degree Limitations

As in any evaluation of alternatives, two points of view exist in the decision of whether or not to obtain an MBA degree. For most graduates, the largest obstacle is obtaining the funds for graduate school. When considering "lost income," in addition to the high cost of education, it becomes tough to justify the expense, particularly if it is coming on the heels of an expensive undergraduate education. Aside from cost considerations, several other disadvantages should be clearly understood.

Many employers hire only bachelor degree candidates and by getting the MBA degree a person might be removing the possibility of consideration for employment. This limitation primarily pertains to the smaller employers which explains why the MBA degree is occasionally criticized for preparing graduates for "big" business.

For many employers the MBA degree is just not required to do the job, and these employers seem reluctant to pay the going salary for the degree. Other employers start the MBA's in relatively the same positions as they do bachelor degree candidates. Imagine the embarrassment to both the employer and the MBA that occurs when the real bright undergraduate outproduces the sharp MBA!

The MBA graduate often has high expectations which may be thwarted shortly after being thrust into an actual job situation. Expectations and career progress do not always stay in step, and it is occasionally a traumatic shock to learn the truth. Actual business experience prior to graduate school is helpful in understanding this fact.

Some undergraduates are "tired" of school but feel they must continue because of the many fears and tales of never returning once a person has left the academic world. This attitude can really hurt. For those who fall into this "tired" category, they should take the prudent course and tackle something new for two or three years. Students who force themselves into a graduate program often do only "average" work. Average and marginal MBA's have a very difficult time seeking employment because the employers are willing to pay for only the outstanding MBA talent. MBA selection and screening criteria will become much keener in the future.

Recruiting Problems

Most people should consider going into business before obtaining the MBA degree. If they find out that the degree is necessary, they can always return to school. This will enable the employed person to find out how important the degree is in the area of interest being pursued.

During the early and mid-sixties the MBA degree grew extremely popular with employers seeking bright, young, potential executive talent. At some points, it even appeared that the MBA degree had a certain charisma associated with it. Starting rates skyrocketed. But the 1970-73 era produced a decline of over 40% in the number of offers. Some experts question whether the "super demand" for the MBA will return.

The MBA degree program normally involves a two-year commitment which means that the cost is something over $20,000 (cost plus lost income). However, starting rates of MBA's are $1,500-$2,000 per year more than those of the bachelor candidates.

Assuming that the MBA is declining in popularity with employers (this may or may not be a true statement), what are some of the reasons? The explanations below have been offered by some employers.

The salary requirements have forced many employers out of the market. The salary difference between a B.S. and MBA is not worth it to many employers.

Business is attracting more top caliber bachelor degree candidates who used to go on to graduate school. Many faculty members no longer automatically encourage their better students to continue study because of the poor job market for advanced degree holders.

Military officer returnees and limited experience job changers are supplying more mature talent. Some top caliber professional employment agencies have opened offices outside major military release bases and have encouraged employers to buy their services.

Other agencies are aiming at the market where young people have less than three years experience. For a salary range between that of a B.S. and MBA, an employer obtains an experienced, 25-30 year old, with leadership potential.

Some employers visit only select MBA schools. The "top ranked" MBA schools experience aggressive recruiting while many other schools are bypassed. About 15 major graduate business schools are highly courted, thus leaving talented MBA's in less prestigious schools searching for jobs on their own. Often, even at the top schools, students in the lower quartile of their class cannot find employment.

The quality of some MBA programs is declining. A rash of new MBA degree programs has proliferated and this has opened wide choices and alternatives to undergraduates. Admission standards may have been bent at many schools to encourage advancement of the program size.

Types of Programs

A large number of universities now offer the Master of Business Administration degree, but not all programs are alike. The differences may be narrowed to the following approaches.

Case Methods. The majority of the courses follow the class structure of solving general or specific problems through use of actual business situations. Those who are strong in class participation should do well.

Quantitative Methods. Curriculums normally follow a pattern of adapting analytical approaches to most business problems regardless of the functional area. Those with a good mathematics and statistics background should do well.

Behavioral Approach. These programs relate the wide variety of business problems to the interrelationships developed between people or groups in the organization or society. Those with a good psychology or sociology background should do well.

Combinations. The majority of programs do offer some combination of the above basic approaches. This requires a well-rounded background in many different subjects.

LAW SCHOOL

In an earlier chapter, it was pointed out in a report by the U.S. Department of Labor that the supply of law graduates in the foreseeable future is likely to far exceed the demand for their services. Yet, the law school offers one of the more popular graduate programs on campuses. Apparently, many students, correctly or incorrectly, believe that law training is a good background for many types of careers. On the average, over 30,000 law graduates will earn degrees each year during the next decade but less than 15,000 are likely to obtain career related types of employment. The picture may get much worse.

Law has always been a venerable and respected profession. The foundation of the American legal system is the common law of England: legislative acts, court precedents, and procedures. Of the nation's 360,000 attorneys, more than 200,000 are engaged in private practice. Of the remainder, about 40,000 are in government service, including 10,000 judges, and the rest are in business fields and other fields such as stock brokerage, banking, teaching, and politics.

A lawyer studies existing laws, interprets them, and advises clients regarding their financial and legal problems. Many attorneys spend a considerable amount of time in courts and preparing research to use in the courts. Others concentrate on preparing legal documents such as property titles, mortgages, contracts, wills, and trust agreements. A lawyer may spend considerable time reading government regulations and ordinances and researching thousands of prior court cases. Some lawyers specialize in criminal cases, real estate, taxes, trusts, corporate law, and other areas.

The Job Market

In 1972, a committee of the American Bar Association made the following report:

> ". . . the recent increase in the number of law students may make dislocations and maldistributions more likely . . . in the future . . . the Association should inform prospective makers of the legal profession. . . . This information will permit law students to formulate reasonable career goals."

The report questions whether the profession can absorb the number of graduates being produced into its ranks. Given these statistics, it would seem wise for individuals to attend the best school they can get into and then work for grades that would rank them near the top in their class.

Salary Information

Records of the Professional Career Development Department of the ABA reveal a broad range of lawyer income. In 1973, starting salaries ranged from $7,000 in small firms to $17,000 in the prestigious New York firms with an average of about $11,000 for those who received employment. With the supply-demand situation, starting salaries are not expected to increase drastically.

Nearly one-third of the profession is currently salaried as associates in law firms, government agencies, or employees in corporations. The others must depend upon fees that vary from year to year depending upon the amount and type of work in which they are involved.

Admission Standards

The standards for admission to any of the 150 plus law schools are high. The Law School Admissions Test is required and about a 600 test score and a grade point average over 3.5 is necessary for admission to the better law schools. The ABA does not rank law schools, but member firms sometimes do, so by checking with several law professors it is possible to learn which schools enjoy the top reputations.

The best jobs go to graduates from the most prestigious schools who rank in the top 10% of their graduating class. Periodically, the ABA publishes a booklet entitled, *Law Schools and Bar Admission Requirements,* which should be reviewed before selecting a school. Many practitioners recommend choosing a law school in the state in which the lawyer is planning to practice.

LAW SCHOOL OR BUSINESS SCHOOL?

Many graduates ponder whether to attend law school or business school. The choice largely depends upon the type of work eventually desired. Both are excellent and prestigious degree to possess, but different avenues are opened by completing each degree. As a guide, the following list of initial starting assignments will indicate some career paths available to graduates with the respective degrees:

MBA Degree

Marketing Programs
Financial Programs
Manufacturing Training
Retailing Programs
Public Accounting
Investment Programs
Business Analysis

JD Degree

Attorney at Law
Labor Relations
Tax Attorney
Patent Lawyer
Trust (wills, estates, etc.)
Government
Politics

For those who desire to go into business immediately following receipt of their degree, the MBA will probably be the best alternative. For those who wish to practice law for a few years prior to going into business, the law degree is their path.

Few companies hire directly into their legal department, if they are large enough to have one. They prefer legal work experience first. Many business employers use a law firm on a retaining basis to handle their legal activities.

For those who have the background, they can always go into the same functional field for which employers consider MBA's. In most cases, however, they give up working in a field that directly utilizes their legal training. Since the overwhelming majority of top management moves into key positions from the functional fields of accounting, finance, marketing, and manufacturing, the MBA may be wiser as a choice if top management is a major personal goal. On the other hand, for those who enjoy the idea of being the expert in a key field, the JD will be their most productive route. The problem ends with a decision for a particular type of work.

Incidentally, the purpose behind the joint MBA-JD degree programs is directed at attorneys with some business savvy so they can become better partners or independent practitioners. Very few business employers recruit for this degree combination. The few that do are public accounting firms (tax lawyers), industrial relations (contract administration, interpretation, and court cases), banks (trusts and wills), and insurance companies (claims). Executives in manufacturing organizations usually take legal matters to the law firm they have on a retainer basis.

SUMMARY

For those who have *definitely* make the decision to continue on to graduate work (Master's, Doctorate, MBA or LLB), they should probably *not* interview. The reason is simply that their qualifications will change; and until the employer can ascertain their level of competence, they can hardly offer a position because the individual is presently not qualified. If the employer could make the offer, there would be no need to go to graduate school. Interviewing should begin when the individual nears the graduate degree.

If graduate school is only a likely possibility for certain people and not a definite commitment, then by all means, they should explore employment opportunities.

Employers are not counselors, so it is not wise for a person to use the interview to ask about graduate school. If recruiters start giving advice, they are not considering the person for employment. If the position desired is offered, then obviously graduate school was not a requirement for the applicant. If an offer is not made, it could mean that further education is needed or that otherwise the applicant is not qualified for the position. Serious soul searching is then a prime concern for the individual.

In summary, if there is a possibility of not getting accepted to graduate school, deciding not to attend, or continuing part-time, it would be a big mistake not to interview. All placement directors can relate sad stories about this happening every year. No interview—no position.

EPILOGUE

Career planning is built on three key concepts. Self-assessment defines the perimeters within the individual that impact sharply upon career choice. Career exploration evaluates the range of potential career options. Placement starts with a career objective and develops a strategy or plan for turning ideas into reality. The decision-making process is the web that brings together all the factors and creates a feedback loop that permits appropriate compromises based upon reality testing.

A successful career search, given career goals, begins with the preparation of the proper tools. The foremost tool is the resume. Cover letters open doors for interviews. Developing contacts and using them to produce interviews is one of the first steps in obtaining job offers. Offers rarely materialize until after completion of several interviews.

Productive interviewing requires advance planning. The key ingredient in interviewing is preparation. An advance strategy, prior preparation of a presentation, and attention to interview techniques represent the hallmark of preparation. The interview is a goal directed activity for both the employer and interviewee. A two-way open channel of communication develops the type of environment that leads to the goal achievement of both parties. Achieving the level of communication requires a mutual understanding of each other's positions. A common base

permits both parties to ask the proper questions and provide a reasoned response in the context of what is expected.

Career planning does not end upon completion of a college degree and acceptance of career related employment. Career planning is a cyclical event that continues to reoccur as the individual gains a more defined self-concept and processes new career information. The cycle frequently includes a career search which may lead to a career or employer change if the new circumstances warrant the complete cycle.

Career planning involves a continual evaluation of career progress based upon a realistic assessment of job performance. Continued education throughout a lifetime is a likely possibility for many individuals. Completion of a college degree is really preparation in the ability to learn through informal and formal training. If success in life, however defined, is a valued asset to an individual, career planning will be a program played throughout a lifetime. Regardless of the current life status, career planning is a real and meaningful process. Individuals who let their working life roll along without conscious direction neglect an important responsibility.

This book touched a little on philosophy, hard concepts, current outlook, communication, techniques, and some nitty-gritty. The illustrations served to drive home a key point or soften the more esoteric

points. The humor was designed to emphasize points in a subtle way and drive home a given point.

The approach offered readers few new ideas. The attempt assembled together a multitude of experienced techniques that worked successfully for young professionals in the past. The principle theme was sharing ideas that time tests have proven effective instead of reinventing the wheel. The gimmicks were few but the methods, techniques, and strategies are the type from which success is born.

For the career planning neophyte the results should have been enormously helpful. For the old pro who has been down the career planning road in the past, perhaps the organization of the concepts helped bring the big picture into better focus. The beneficial result of even a brief review of the career planning process is that often only one or two new ideas can help turn frustration in the career search to a fruitful exercise.

Critics are invited to share their views with the author. The risk of such sharing is that the new viewpoint may be expressed in the next revision. Authors learn and improve too!